Dear Phoram & Kaushal,

Happy Cooking!

Sanjeev Kapoor's
**the yellow chilli**
Cookbook

*Sanjeev Kapoor*

# Sanjeev Kapoor's
## the yellow chilli
## Cookbook

In association with Alyona Kapoor

PopulaR Prakashan

www.popularprakashan.com

Published by
POPULAR PRAKASHAN PVT. LTD.
301, Mahalaxmi Chambers
22, Bhulabhai Desai Road
Mumbai – 400 026
for KHANA KHAZANA PUBLICATIONS PVT. LTD.

(4416)
ISBN: 978-81-7991-668-1

Editor: Ramya Sarma

Design: Sameer Madye (2 Do Design)

Photography: Vikas Shinde for Sanjeev Kapoor

Part images (other than recipes and restaurant) sourced from Shutterstock.

Food Styling: Anupa Das

Printed in India
by Thomson Press (India) Ltd.
New Delhi

This book is dedicated to

All the patrons of The Yellow Chilli who have appreciated our food
over the years and encouraged and inspired us to keep trying harder

# Author's Note

Some years ago one question was often asked: "Why doesn't Sanjeev Kapoor have his own restaurant? He has a TV show, but why not a restaurant where we can go and eat the food cooked using his recipes?"

The answer came in 2001 with the launch of the very first The Yellow Chilli restaurant in Ludhiana. Today, ten years later, the restaurant has grown threefold and is still Number 1 in the city of Ludhiana.

Soon our dishes - like Lalla Mussa Dal, Chandi Kaliyan, Shaam Savera and Gulab-e-Gulkand - became a roaring success. There has been no looking back since then. Our motto of serving deliciously different food at The Yellow Chilli stands as strong today as it did in 2001 and we do not use colours or additives in our recipes, even though it may be the norm to do so. The Yellow Chilli offers the experience of five star food at three star rates. Our patrons come in with friends and family to enjoy our delicious fare at affordable rates. The same satisfied patrons soon requested us to share The Yellow Chilli recipes with them and thus the seed for this book was sown.

Yes, a book of recipes, because in the printed form they can be handed down through generations. So THE YELLOW CHILLI COOKBOOK went from being just an idea to taking shape as a colourful collection of restaurant recipes in a very short span of time. We hope that making the food presented here can give you the satisfaction that you have cooked with élan and confidence and really 'dined out' in the comfort of your own home!

Another oft-asked question is, 'Why does restaurant food taste different from home cooked?' or 'What is the difference between home cooked food and restaurant food?' To this I would say that the best thing about restaurant food is that you don't have to make it yourself. On the other hand, the best thing about the food that you have cooked yourself is the satisfaction of knowing that you have created the meal. But if you can cook restaurant style food at home, wouldn't it be really satisfying?

Choosing the recipes to go into this collection was not done overnight. We had to survey all the outlets, pull out the dishes that are bestsellers, scale down the recipe perfectly for four portions and then triple-test each. When you cook in large cauldrons, you cook differently. When you cook on super high heat, as is done in commercial kitchens, you cook differently. So adapting the recipes for home use was an enjoyable and educational trip.

You could start your delicious evening with a palate cleansing Tomato Basil Shorba, and accompany it with Khaas Seekh and Royal Hara Bhara. Indulge yourself with extra special Raan Buzkazi and offer Kadai Tandoori Gobhi Mussallam to those who don't eat meat. Pile up Peshawari Naans, and make it all special with Bhindi Raita, a dip with a difference. Then bring the meal to a crescendo with an exotic Gulab-e-Gulkand. Please remember that all portions serve four and are meant to complement other dishes in the meal.

Time to bring out your fine china, special glassware and cutlery and spread out The Yellow Chilli feast for your family. We hope you enjoy the food as much as we enjoyed bringing it to you!

Happy cooking!

*Sanjeev Kapoor*

Sanjeev Kapoor

# The Yellow Chilli
## *an experience to remember*

When we launched 'The Yellow Chilli' brand, the question was, "Why has Sanjeev Kapoor named it 'The Yellow Chilli'? We know about red ones and green ones, but yellow?" Fact is, the yellow chilli does exist.

Chilli – whatever its colour - is almost always loaded with spice. Cut it and it will sting. Nibble it and it will bite back. That works with red chillies and green chillies. For me, the yellow chilli was simply inconceivable. That is, till one fine day a number of years ago I discovered it on the streets of Meerut. As all connoisseurs know, Meerut is the melting pot of unique chaats. The special yellow chilli spice mix that the chaatwallas use here adds that

extra zing and brings together a confluence of flavours, aromas and colours. I have been travelling the length and breadth of India in search of unique tastes and flavours that have provided inspiration for many of my recipes. It took all but one bite and I wanted to use the name in a creative way. And thus 'The Yellow Chilli' came into being. It is certainly not imaginary. And now a nondescript, unimportant little street-food ingredient has its name taken to new heights with the success of 'The Yellow Chilli' as a brand.

The first restaurant was launched in 2001 in Ludhiana and soon outlets in New Delhi, Amritsar, Jalandhar, Panchkula, Noida,

Guwahati, Greater Noida, Saibabad, Ghaziabad, Hyderabad, Pune, Mumbai, Ahmedabad and Bhuj came into being. With every new unit that was established, we learnt something new; we learnt about what people wanted, and our specialty of being flexible stood us in good stead. We have never claimed to be authentic, but cooked what we felt was right, tweaking it to suit the tastes of the local patrons. For a sample, try the Naan Pizza at the The Yellow Chilli in Ahmedabad. The Ahmedabadis love pizza, so we gave it a twist with a base of naan - today it is a bestseller! Other hot favourites in that city are the Roomali Khakra and Indian Sizzlers. In fact, the menu in each unit has a page dedicated to local delights. The outlets at Ahmedabad and Bhuj are the first ever all-vegetarian restaurants. At every unit the main chef is provided and trained by the Sanjeev Kapoor team. Also, the menu at every unit is improved upon every year with frequent auditing and training. The Yellow Chilli logo, too, has gone through a few transformations... but that is all part of growing up! Now the stage is set for new restaurants in Saudi Arabia, Bahrain, Kathmandu, Chandigarh and Kolkata, with many more in the pipeline in the near future.

So when you enter The Yellow Chilli, be assured that it offers you a casual dining experience as THE Indian cuisine restaurant in your neighbourhood. Be assured that you need to spend just around Rs 250-350 per head (without liquor) on food that is not only deliciously different, but also redefines Indian cuisine. The mantra is simple at The Yellow Chilli: a wide range of exclusive recipes with a touch of simplicity, served in immaculate style. The ambience will soothe the eye and the heart and as you are made comfortable in your seat, you can sit back and expect service that will not only impress you, but also inspire you to tell friends about your overall experience and the delightful meal you ate at The Yellow Chilli. The Yellow Chilli brand will continue to strive to exceed the expectations of every guest and empower more entrepreneurs along its journey into the future.

Enjoy the pampering that is rightfully yours when you step into The Yellow Chilli restaurant, because here - though the food is king - it is you, our guest, who is the emperor.

# Contents

## Non Vegetarian Main Course

## Rice & Rotis

## Dals & Accompaniments

## Sweets

# Aperitif

# Aperitif

# Murgh Yakhni

Chicken soup is considered good for the soul and for the body, but this one, subtly flavoured with fennel and ginger, is uber-delicious. One of the most popular and fast moving aperitifs in our restaurant, it provides me an immense boost, especially after a stressful day. The garnish of fried spinach strips makes it look very appetising indeed. While working on this recipe, in the initial stages we did try using roasted besan as the thickener, but it did not work to our satisfaction.

## Ingredients

3 cups chicken stock

100 grams boneless chicken breast, boiled and chopped into ½ inch cubes

1 tablespoon butter

2 medium onions, chopped

2 tablespoons yogurt, whisked

1 tablespoon refined flour (maida)

2 garlic cloves, chopped

1 teaspoon fennel seeds (saunf)

8 black peppercorns

2 black cardamoms

4 green cardamoms

2 bay leaves

Salt to taste

2 inch ginger piece, chopped

2-3 fresh spinach leaves, cut into thin strips and deep fried

## Method

1. Heat butter in a deep non stick pan, add onions and sauté till golden.

2. Add yogurt and mix well and cook till the moisture evaporates.

3. Add refined flour and mix well and sauté for a couple of minutes.

4. Add garlic, fennel seeds, peppercorns, black cardamoms, green cardamoms and bay leaves and mix well. Add chicken stock and stir, ensuring there are no lumps. Simmer on low heat for fifteen minutes.

5. Add salt and ginger and mix. Cook for five minutes or till the mixture reduces slightly.

6. Strain into a soup bowl, garnish with fried spinach strips and chicken cubes and serve hot.

# Jau Aur Subziyon Ka Shorba

With healthy eating being the order of the day, we introduced this shorba - it became an instant hit with our regular patrons. Easy to make and delicious, the combination of barley, well packed with nutrition, and plenty of vegetables makes the shorba hearty and wholesome. Even after cooking, the barley stays somewhat chewy and has a pleasant, nutty taste and a nice mouth feel.

## Ingredients

1 cup pearl barley (jau)

1 teaspoon oil

2 tablespoons butter

20-22 garlic cloves, chopped

1½ inch ginger piece, grated

1 medium onion, chopped

1 tablespoon black peppercorns

7-8 bay leaves

10-12 French beans, finely chopped

¾ medium carrot, finely chopped

3 large florets of broccoli, finely chopped

2 large florets of cauliflower, finely chopped

Salt to taste

20 fresh coriander stems

## Method

1. Wash the barley well and drain thoroughly.  Heat the oil in a non stick pan, add the barley and sauté till lightly browned and dry. Transfer into a bowl, add two cups water and let it soak overnight.

2. Heat the butter in a deep non stick pan. Add the garlic and ginger and sauté for a minute.  Add the onion and sauté on medium heat for four to six minutes or till the onion turns translucent.

3. Drain and add the barley and sauté for five minutes. Add the black peppercorns and bay leaves and sauté for five minutes more.

4. Keeping aside a little of the French beans, carrot and broccoli, add the rest to the pan along with cauliflower and mix.  Add salt and sauté for two minutes.

5. Add coriander stems and five litres of water and let it come to a boil on high heat. Simmer for at least twenty to twenty five minutes or till it is reduced to half its original quantity.

6. Strain the soup into another deep non stick pan. Add the reserved French beans, carrot and broccoli and cook for five to seven minutes.

7. Serve piping hot.

# Kesar Elaichi Lassi

Cooling aperitifs such as this delectable lassi make for a wonderful start to the delicious fare to follow. Some people, however, like to end their meals with a tall glass of this cool drink. The choice is yours, a personal preference. One tip: you should be very careful while buying saffron and always look for the 'organic' label for there is a lot of adulterated stuff available in the market. Remember, buying saffron is almost like buying gold

## Ingredients

A few strands of saffron

½ teaspoon green cardamom powder

4 cups yogurt, whisked

⅔ cup + 1 tablespoon warm milk

1 tablespoon rose syrup

10 tablespoons powdered sugar

A few ice cubes

4 pedas, crushed

4 tablespoons rabdi

10-12 almonds, slivered

10-12 pistachios, slivered

## Method

1.  Soak saffron in one tablespoon of warm milk and set aside.

2.  Combine yogurt and the remaining warm milk in a bowl and blend with a hand blender.

3.  Add green cardamom powder, rose syrup and powdered sugar and blend some more.

4.  Add saffron milk and mix.  Add ice cubes and stir.

5.  Pour into individual glasses, add crushed pedas and rabdi on top.  Garnish with slivered almonds and pistachios and serve chilled.

# Tomato Basil Shorba

## Ingredients

6 medium tomatoes, roughly chopped

7 garlic cloves

1 inch cinnamon stick

1 black cardamom

½ tablespoon black peppercorns

1 tablespoon cumin seeds

2 dried red chillies

½ cup chopped fresh coriander stems

3-4 basil stems

1 teaspoon oil

½ teaspoon red chilli (deghi mirch) powder

2 tablespoons gram flour (besan)

½ tablespoon lemon juice

Pesto for garnish

6-8 fresh basil leaves

3 garlic cloves

4 cashewnuts

4 tablespoons oil

Say 'soup' and people think of tomato. But we wanted to give tomato soup lovers something extra. So we added basil and look what we got – a soup with healthy herbal flavour! Food is all about sensation, appreciation, digestion, all linked together and working as one. And Indian food, in particular, is bright, vivid, sharp, beautiful – in aroma, colour, appearance, taste and effect. Deghi mirch is one additive that brings out all these qualities, adding brilliant colour rather than heat, making the food more appetising to look at and so to taste. But be extra careful with it though, since more than the specified amount can ruin an absolutely perfect soup.

## Method

1. Combine the tomatoes, garlic, cinnamon, cardamom, peppercorns, cumin seeds, red chillies, coriander stems, basil stems, five cups of water and oil in a deep non stick pan and boil for ten to twelve minutes.

2. Add red chilli powder and mix. Take the pan off the heat and strain into another deep non stick pan.

3. Add one cup water and boil it for five minutes.

4. Roast gram flour in another non stick pan for four to five minutes or till fragrant. Add half cup water and mix well. Add this to shorba and boil for five minutes.

5. To make the pesto, grind together basil leaves, garlic, cashewnuts with oil to a smooth paste.

6. Add lemon juice to the shorba and mix. Serve hot garnished with pesto.

# Khasta Chaat Bites

We were hopeful that this idea to serve stuffed patties chaat style would be well received, but its success was way beyond our collective imagination! It can be a complete meal by itself – it's so filling and wholesome.

## Ingredients

**For pattice**

4 medium potatoes
A pinch of nutmeg powder
Salt to taste
1½ tablespoons cornflour
Oil for shallow frying

**For stuffing**

¼ cup split skinless black gram (dhuli urad dal), soaked
A pinch of turmeric powder
2 green chillies, chopped
½ inch ginger piece, chopped
1 teaspoon red chilli powder
1 teaspoon chaat masala
¼ cup chopped fresh coriander leaves
A pinch of asafoetida

**For serving**

1 cup yogurt
1 tablespoon powdered sugar
A few drops of rose water
2 tablespoons sweet date and tamarind chutney
½ tablespoon green chutney
¼ teaspoon roasted cumin powder
A pinch of black salt
¼ teaspoon chaat masala
¼ teaspoon Kashmiri red chilli powder
8 papdis, crushed
1 small beetroot, cut into thin strips, soaked in chilled water and drained
Pickled carrot strips (see note below)
¼ cup fine sev
¼ cup fresh pomegranate pearls
¼ cup khari boondi
A few sprigs of fresh coriander leaves

## Method

1. Place the potatoes in a vessel and cover with a lid. Pour three cups water in a large pressure cooker and place a stand in it. On this stand put the vessel containing the potatoes. Cook under pressure till pressure is released four to five times (four to five whistles). Open the lid when pressure reduces completely and remove the potatoes. Cool, peel and grate.

2. Alternatively, wash potatoes well and while still damp, cook them in microwave oven at 100% for ten minutes.

3. Place the grated potatoes in a bowl, add nutmeg, salt, cornflour and mix well. Divide into four equal portions.

4. For the stuffing, boil the urad dal with a pinch of turmeric powder and one cup water for eight minutes. Drain well, transfer into a bowl and let it cool.

5. Add green chillies, ginger, red chilli powder, chaat masala, coriander leaves, asafoetida and salt and mix well. Divide into four equal portions.

6. Stuff each portion of potato mixture with a portion of urad dal mixture and seal well. Shape them into tikkis.

7. Heat sufficient oil in a non stick pan and shallow-fry the tikkis, turning over, till both sides are golden. Drain on absorbent paper.

8. Mix yogurt and powdered sugar well.

9. Keep each tikki on a separate plate, pour some yogurt over it. Sprinkle with rose water and drizzle date and tamarind chutney and green chutney. Over this sprinkle cumin powder, black salt, chaat masala and red chilli powder. Top with crushed papdis, beetroot strips, pickled carrot strips, sev, pomegranate pearls and khari boondi. Garnish with a coriander sprig and serve immediately.

Note  To make pickled carrot strips, cut one small carrot into thin strips and keep it soaked in half cup of vinegar for half an hour.

# Three Chilli Potato Salad

Don't get misled by the name - this dish is not all that spicy, since the 'chillies' refers to three coloured capsicums and not Kashmiri red chilli, peppercorns and chilli flakes. In fact, we initially had a tough time making our chefs understand that! It's so very delicious that I am often tempted to make a full meal of this salad. At our restaurants too it has caught on big time.

## Ingredients

32-34 baby potatoes, boiled and peeled

¾ teaspoon turmeric powder

1½ teaspoons red chilli powder

Salt to taste

1 teaspoon black pepper powder

2 tablespoons oil

1 medium red capsicum, thickly sliced

1 medium yellow capsicum, thickly sliced

1 medium green capsicum, thickly sliced

1 medium tomato, seeded and thickly sliced

1 medium onion, thickly sliced and layers separated

2 tablespoons tomato ketchup

½ tablespoon tamarind pulp

1 teaspoon chaat masala

1 tablespoon lemon juice

1 teaspoon crushed black peppercorns

1 sprig fresh coriander leaves

1 lemon, cut into wedges

## Method

1. Preheat oven to 250°C / 475°F.

2. Mix together turmeric powder, red chilli powder, salt, black pepper powder and oil. Apply this paste to the potatoes and place them in a baking tray and bake in the preheated oven for ten to fifteen minutes. Remove from the oven and set aside to cool.

3. Transfer the potatoes into a bowl, add red capsicum, yellow capsicum, green capsicum, tomato and onion and mix well.

4. Add tomato ketchup, tamarind pulp, chaat masala, salt, lemon juice and crushed black peppercorns and mix well.

5. Serve cold garnished with coriander sprigs and lemon wedges.

# Vegetarian Starters

# Vegetarian Starters

# Pashtuni Chana Tikki

Adapted from the North West Frontier cuisine, we have given these tikkis our own twist. Absolutely mouth-watering! You just have to taste a piece once and you will definitely ask for more, just the way Oliver Twist did.

## Ingredients

1¼ cups (250 grams) chickpeas (kabuli chana), soaked overnight

2 teaspoons tea leaves

12 pieces dried Indian gooseberry (amla)

3 green cardamoms

1 black cardamom

2 bay leaves

1 inch cinnamon stick

1 medium potato, boiled, peeled and mashed

1 tablespoon coriander powder

2 teaspoons Kashmiri red chilli powder

Salt to taste

1 tablespoon lemon juice

4 tablespoons chopped fresh coriander leaves

4 green chillies, finely chopped

1½ inch ginger piece, chopped

1 teaspoon chholay masala (see annexure)

1 teaspoon chaat masala (see annexure)

1 teaspoon dried mango powder (amchur)

12 cashewnuts, chopped

2 tablespoons raisins, chopped

Oil for shallow frying

For serving

Mint chutney, as required

1 large onion, finely sliced

## Method

1. Drain the chickpeas and put in a pressure cooker. Tie up the tea leaves, amla, green cardamoms, black cardamom, bay leaves and cinnamon in a muslin cloth to make a potli and add to the cooker along with five cups of water. Cover the cooker with the lid and keep on low heat, till pressure is released eight to ten times (eight to ten whistles).

2. Open the lid when the pressure reduces completely, discard the spice potli, strain the chickpeas and reserve the cooking liquour, which can be used in some other dish.

3. Mince the boiled chickpeas. Transfer into a bowl and add potato, coriander powder, Kashmiri red chilli powder, salt, lemon juice, two tablespoons coriander leaves and mix well together.

4. Add the green chillies and ginger and mix well. Add the chholay masala, chaat masala and amchur and mix well.

5. For the stuffing, mix together the cashewnuts, raisins and the remaining coriander leaves.

6. Divide the chickpea mixture and the stuffing into twelve portions each.

7. Stuff each chickpea portion with a portion of the stuffing and shape into a tikki.

8. Heat a little oil on a non stick pan and shallow fry the tikkis four at a time, turning a few times till golden on both sides.

9. Drain on absorbent paper. Serve hot with mint chutney and onion.

# Aloo Nazakat

## Ingredients

5 large potatoes, peeled

Oil for deep frying

For the marinade

1 tablespoon oil

½ teaspoon turmeric powder

2 tablespoons red chilli powder

¾ teaspoon Khazana garam masala powder (see annexure)

1 tablespoon roasted gram flour (besan)

½ cup hung yogurt

Salt to taste

½ teaspoon dried fenugreek leaves (kasoori methi)

¼ tablespoon ginger paste

½ tablespoon garlic paste

¼ teaspoon green chilli paste

For the stuffing

½ cup grated cottage cheese (paneer)

¾ inch ginger piece, chopped

1 tablespoon chopped fresh coriander leaves

1 tablespoon chopped fresh mint leaves

10 raisins, chopped

6 fried and crushed cashewnuts

½ teaspoon red chilli power

¾ teaspoon chaat masala (see annexure)

Salt to taste

½ teaspoon cumin powder

There is nothing more delightful than the partnership of potatoes, oil and spices. Aloo Nazakat is one of our three top selling vegetarian starters at our restaurant. It is not a traditional potato dish, but a creative one. When potatoes are deep fried, the calorie-conscious brain cells may shriek with horror, but the soul starts a little dance of joy as the mouth bites into a crisp outer casing that yields to soft, warm, fluffy starch inside. Judging by its popularity, in a few decades this dish could easily be counted in the top 100 Indian foods that people remember.

## Method

1. Preheat oven to 250ºC/ 475ºF.
2. Slice off a thin slice from the top of four potatoes and scoop out the centre to give a barrel shape. Keep the trimmings aside. Halve the remaining potato. Blanch the potatoes in boiling water for ten minutes. Drain thoroughly.
3. Heat sufficient oil in a kadai and deep fry the potato barrels, one half of the fifth potato and the trimmings separately till light golden. Drain on absorbent paper. Mash the trimmings and the half potato and set aside.
4. For the marinade heat the oil in a non stick pan. Remove the pan from heat and add the turmeric powder, red chilli powder, garam masala powder, roasted gram flour and mix well. Add this to hung yogurt along with salt, kasoori methi, ginger paste, garlic paste and green chilli paste to make a smooth mixture.
5. For the stuffing mix together the grated paneer, fried and mashed fried potato, ginger, coriander leaves, mint leaves, raisins, cashewnuts, red chilli powder, chaat masala, salt and cumin powder.
6. Stuff this mixture into the fried potatoes. Coat the potatoes with the marinade and arrange them upright on a baking tray. Bake them in the preheated oven for fifteen minutes.
7. Serve hot.

# Arbi Ke Khaje

Arbis are sticky to handle, but frying in oil makes them easier to handle – the vegetable not only holds its shape, but gets non-sticky, making it easier to coat it with masala. On many occasions our guest book gets the comment: 'Could not believe that I had such amazing arbi!'

## Ingredients

16 (approximately 415 grams) colocassia roots (arbi), boiled and peeled

1 tablespoon oil + for deep frying

¾ cup cornflour

Salt to taste

2 teaspoons Kashmiri red chilli powder

1 teaspoon dried mango powder (amchur)

1 teaspoon cumin powder

1 teaspoon coriander powder

1 teaspoon chaat masala (see annexure)

4 green chillies, chopped

20 curry leaves

**To serve**

Mint chutney, as required

## Method

1. Heat oil in a kadai.
2. Sift together the cornflour, salt and one teaspoon red chilli powder onto a plate.
3. Press the arbi between your palms and coat them with the above mixture. Slide them into the hot oil and deep fry on medium heat till golden and crisp. Drain on absorbent paper and set aside.
4. Mix together the remaining red chilli powder, amchur, cumin powder, coriander powder, chaat masala and salt in a bowl.
5. Heat one tablespoon oil in a non stick pan, add green chillies and curry leaves and sauté for two minutes. Add the fried arbi and the mixed masala powders and toss well so that all the arbi pieces are well coated with the masala.
6. Serve hot with mint chutney.

# Hara Masaley Ka Bhuna Paneer

## Ingredients

275 grams cottage cheese (paneer), cut into 16 one-inch squares

¼ cup fresh coriander leaf paste

¼ cup fresh mint leaf paste

¼ cup fresh spinach puree

1 tablespoon green chilli paste

1½ tablespoons oil

½ teaspoon mustard seeds

10-12 curry leaves

1 teaspoon turmeric powder

1 teaspoon Kashmiri red chilli powder

1 teaspoon Khazana garam masala powder

2 tablespoons roasted gram flour (besan)

½ cup yogurt

Salt to taste

½ teaspoon black salt

1 teaspoon cumin powder

2 teaspoons chaat masala

1 tablespoon lemon juice

1 medium green capsicum, cut into 1 inch pieces

1 medium onion, cut into 1 inch pieces

2 medium tomatoes, cut into 1 inch pieces

Butter for basting

**For garnish**

1 medium onion, cut into rings

1 lemon, cut into wedges

1 sprig fresh coriander leaves

Paneer starters are common in most restaurants. But this one is a visual delight. It has paneer smothered in green chutney and baked on skewers with onions, capsicums and tomatoes. Softer the paneer even better the result, but be wary of handling the cheese too much lest it breaks and makes things difficult.

## Method

1. Heat the oil in a non stick pan and add the mustard seeds. When they splutter, remove the pan from heat, add the curry leaves, turmeric powder, Kashmiri red chilli powder and Khazana garam masala powder and mix well.

2. Transfer this mixture onto a flat plate. Add the roasted gram flour and yogurt and mix well. Add the coriander leaf paste, mint leaf paste, spinach puree and green chilli paste and mix well.

3. Add the salt, black salt, cumin powder, one teaspoon chaat masala and lemon juice and mix again.

4. Add the paneer pieces and mix well so that all the pieces are well coated with the masala. Set aside to marinate for half an hour.

5. Preheat oven to 250°C / 475°F.

6. Thread onto skewers in this order: capsicum, paneer, tomato, paneer, onion, paneer, capsicum, paneer and lastly onion. Thread three more skewers in the same sequence.

7. Place the skewers on a baking tray and cook in the oven, basting with butter in between, for eight to ten minutes.

8. Remove from the oven, sprinkle the remaining chaat masala over them and serve hot garnished with onion rings, lemon wedges and sprigs of fresh coriander.

# Shahi Subz Seekh

## Ingredients

⅓ medium carrot, grated

2 florets of cauliflower, grated

¼ cup American corn, blanched and minced

¼ cup shelled green peas, blanched and minced

1 small potato, boiled, peeled and grated

¼ cup boiled and grated yam (suran)

5 French beans, finely chopped

1 tablespoon oil

⅓ tablespoon caraway seeds (shahi jeera)

⅓ teaspoon turmeric powder

⅓ tablespoon coriander powder

½ tablespoon cumin powder

⅓ tablespoon Khazana garam masala powder (see annexure)

A pinch of green cardamom powder

Salt to taste

1 tablespoon cashewnut powder

⅔ tablespoon roasted chana powder

2 teaspoons oil

8 satay sticks, soaked

To serve

1 large onion, cut into rings

Mint chutney, as required

The Indian meal is made far more appetizing when it proceeds slowly, progressing through many courses and punctuated with conversation and munchies. One such easy to eat and delicious food is the seekh kebab. Kababs are a gift of the Mughal era and are considered to be perfect when the meat is melt-in-the-mouth tender, the spices leaving the palate asking for more. The challenge comes with the vegetarian versions, where the base ingredient holds the main responsibility of making or marring the kabab. When work on this recipe was in progress, we were faced with the problem of choosing softness of the kabab over strength of the binding. Finally, softness won the battle.

## Method

1. Heat the oil in a non stick wok, add the caraway seeds and turmeric powder and sauté.

2. Add the carrot, cauliflower, corn, green peas, potato, yam and French beans and sauté on medium heat for ten minutes.

3. Add the coriander powder, cumin powder, garam masala powder, green cardamom powder and salt and mix well.

4. Reduce heat, add the cashewnut powder and roasted chana powder and mix well. Sauté till all the moisture dries up. Remove from heat and set aside to cool.

5. Preheat oven to 220ºC / 440ºF. Grease a baking tray with the oil.

6. Divide the mixture into twelve equal portions and pat each portion onto a satay stick to make a slim cylinder. Place these on a greased baking tray.

7. Cook in the preheated oven for five to eight minutes or till golden brown.

8. Serve hot with the onion rings and mint chutney.

# Shabnam Ke Moti

The name itself spells romance – Shabnam ke Moti. This is a starter made with button mushrooms stuffed with a spicy paneer mixture and made extra special by coating each with rich cheese layer before baking to golden perfection.

## Ingredients

8 large button mushrooms

4 wooden satay sticks, soaked

**For coating**

¼ cup grated processed cheese

¼ cup hung yogurt

½ teaspoon green cardamom powder

¼ teaspoon white pepper powder

¼ teaspoon Khazana garam masala powder (see annexure)

¼ teaspoon ginger paste

¼ teaspoon garlic paste

½ teaspoon green chilli paste

½ tablespoon cornflour

**For haldi rogan**

1 teaspoon oil

A large pinch of turmeric powder

**For stuffing**

¼ cup grated cottage cheese (paneer)

1 tablespoon chopped fresh coriander leaves

¼ inch ginger piece, chopped

½ tablespoon chopped fresh mint leaves

1 green chilli, chopped

Salt to taste

**To serve**

Sweet date and tamarind chutney

Mint chutney

## Method

1. Remove the stems of the mushrooms and blanch the tops in boiling water for five minutes. Drain thoroughly.

2. Preheat oven to 250°C / 475°F.

3. For the coating, mash the cheese well in a flat plate. Add the hung yogurt and mix well. Add the green cardamom powder, white pepper powder, garam masala powder, ginger paste, garlic paste, green chilli paste and cornflour and mix well.

4. To make haldi rogan, heat the oil in a small non stick pan, add the turmeric powder and take the pan off the heat. Add this to the cheese mixture and mix well.

5. For the stuffing, mix together the paneer, coriander leaves, ginger, mint leaves, green chilli and salt.

6. Fill all the mushrooms with this stuffing. Place one mushroom over the other, open end facing each other, and string them onto a satay stick. Prepare the remaining mushrooms similarly. Coat with the cheese mixture and arrange them on a baking tray. Bake in the preheated oven for fifteen minutes.

7. Serve hot with sweet date and tamarind chutney and mint chutney.

# Royal Hara Bhara

## Ingredients

2 bunches (660 grams) fresh spinach, blanched and pureed

2 medium green capsicums, roughly chopped

2 cups chopped spring onion greens

4 green chillies

2 tablespoons oil + for shallow frying

1½ tablespoons caraway seeds (shahi jeera)

¾ teaspoon turmeric powder

2 tablespoons ginger paste

2 tablespoons garlic paste

1 tablespoon green chilli paste

1 teaspoon coriander powder

1 teaspoon green cardamom powder

1½ teaspoons Khazana garam masala powder

3 tablespoons crushed cashewnuts

Salt to taste

1 teaspoon chaat masala

2 tablespoons roasted gram flour (besan)

Green chutney, as required

### For stuffing

8 tablespoons hung yogurt

2 green chillies, chopped

1 tablespoon chopped pickled ginger

2 tablespoons chopped almonds

1 teaspoon chaat masala

¾ teaspoon Khazana garam masala powder

The watchword these days is 'Go green'. And what better way to do just that than include lots of green foods in your diet? Hara Bhara kababs are essentially a dish made popular by most Indian restaurants as a vegetarian starter. But at The Yellow Chilli, we make it a little complex and stuff it with yogurt and ginger. And that's what makes it fit for royalty. Before launching this starter, we were faced with the dilemma: serve it shallow fried or deep fried? The healthier version won.

## Method

1. Grind together the green capsicums, spring onion greens and green chillies.

2. Heat two tablespoons of oil in a non stick pan and add caraway seeds. When they change colour, add the turmeric powder and mix. Add the ginger and garlic pastes and sauté for a minute.

3. Add the green chilli paste and sauté for three minutes. Add the ground paste and sauté for three to four minutes. Add the spinach puree and cook, stirring, till dry.

4. Add the coriander powder, green cardamom powder, garam masala powder, crushed cashewnuts, salt and chaat masala and mix well. Set aside to cool.

5. Add the roasted gram flour and mix well.

6. For the stuffing, mix together the hung yogurt, green chillies, ginger, almonds, chaat masala and garam masala powder.

7. Divide the spinach mixture into sixteen equal portions. Take each portion in your palm and shape it into a small katori, fill it with the stuffing, bring in the edges to enclose it completely. Shape into a ball and press lightly to flatten it.

8. Heat sufficient oil on a non stick tawa, place half the kababs on it and shallow fry, turning sides, till crisp on both sides. Cook the remaining kababs in the same way.

9. Serve hot with green chutney.

# Phaldari Akhrot Kakori

## Ingredients

200 grams cauliflower, separated into florets and boiled

25 French beans, boiled

2 medium carrots, grated

2 medium potatoes, boiled, peeled and mashed

4 raw bananas, boiled, peeled and mashed

2 tablespoons butter + for brushing

1 tablespoon caraway seeds (shahi jeera)

7-8 garlic cloves, chopped

1 tablespoon green chilli paste

4 green chillies, chopped

1 inch ginger piece, cut into thin strips

1 tablespoon cumin powder

1 tablespoon coriander powder

A pinch of clove powder

½ cup grated khoya/mawa

100 grams cottage cheese (paneer), grated

1½ tablespoons green cardamom powder

1½ cups cashewnut powder

1 teaspoon Khazana garam masala powder (see annexure)

Salt to taste

4 tablespoons roasted chana dal powder

20-22 walnut kernels, crushed

¼ cup raisins, chopped

Walnuts not only add their nutrient content to this extremely delicious kabab, they also give it that extra crunchiness. It does require quite a bit of labour to mince all those vegetables – but then the fruits of labour are always delicious. I like to serve this at my house parties and the guests never stop at one.

## Method

1. Mince the cauliflower, French beans and carrots in a mincer.

2. Heat the butter in a non stick wok, add caraway seeds, garlic and green chilli paste and sauté on medium heat for five minutes.

3. Add potatoes, raw bananas and the minced vegetables and mix well. Cook for five to ten minutes on medium heat.

4. Add chopped green chillies, ginger strips, cumin powder, coriander powder, clove powder, khoya, paneer, green cardamom powder, cashewnut powder, garam masala powder and salt and cook for five minutes.

5. Add roasted chana dal powder and cook for five minutes more. Add half the walnuts and raisins and cook for five minutes. Take the pan off the heat and set aside to cool.

6. Preheat the oven to 250°C/ 475°F.

7. Divide the mixture into eight equal portions and roll each portion into a five inch long cylinder.

8. Coat them with the remaining walnuts and place them on a greased tray. Cook in the preheated oven for five to seven minutes.

9. Remove them from the oven, brush with butter and serve hot.

# Non-vegetarian Starters

# Non-vegetarian Starters

# Murgh Angaar Bedgi

As the name suggests, this dish is high on chilli heat. Pieces of boneless chicken marinated in yogurt and bedgi chillies are cooked in the oven on skewers. This one could make you sniffle a bit, but you will invariably reach for more of the stuff that 'tastes better than any tikka in the world'.

## Ingredients

400 grams boneless chicken, cut into 16 pieces

3 teaspoons garlic paste

1½ teaspoons ginger paste

3½ teaspoons lemon juice

2 tablespoons Kashmiri red chilli paste

3 teaspoons Kashmiri red chilli powder

Salt to taste

1½ tablespoons oil

¼ teaspoon carom seeds (ajwain)

½ tablespoon gram flour (besan)

½ teaspoon turmeric powder

½ teaspoon Khazana garam masala powder (see annexure)

½ cup yogurt

1 teaspoon red chilli flakes

½ teaspoon black salt

Butter for basting

1 teaspoon chaat masala (see annexure)

1 lemon, cut into wedges

## Method

1.  Mix two teaspoons garlic paste, one teaspoon ginger paste, two teaspoons lemon juice, two tablespoons red chilli paste, one teaspoon red chilli powder and salt in a bowl. Add the chicken pieces and mix well. Set aside in a refrigerator to marinate for thirty minutes.

2.  Heat the oil in a small non stick pan. Add the carom seeds and remove the pan from the heat. Add the gram flour and mix well. Add the turmeric powder, three fourth tablespoon red chilli powder and garam masala powder and mix. Add this to the yogurt and mix till smooth.

3.  Add the red chilli flakes, one teaspoon garlic paste, half teaspoon ginger paste, salt, black salt and half tablespoon lemon juice and mix well.

4.  Add the marinated chicken pieces and mix well. Set aside in the refrigerator to marinate for thirty minutes more.

5.  Preheat oven to 250ºC / 475ºF.

6.  String the chicken pieces onto skewers and cook in the preheated oven for ten minutes.

7.  Remove from the oven, baste with butter and cook for ten minutes more.

8.  Remove the chicken pieces from the skewers and arrange them on a serving plate, sprinkle with chaat masala and serve hot with lemon wedges.

# Khaas Seekh

This is a special kabab on a skewer that requires a little finesse in assembling it but cooking is done in a jiffy...the best part of these kababs is that you can prepare them in advance and keep under a cling wrap in the refrigerator. Cook them just before serving. You will enjoy comments like 'astonishing piece of art'!

## Ingredients

400 grams minced chicken (keema)

¾ inch ginger piece, chopped

15 garlic cloves, chopped

1½ green chillies, chopped

Salt to taste

1½ teaspoons green cardamom powder

1 teaspoon white pepper powder

2 teaspoons ghee

100 grams grated cottage cheese (paneer)

3 tablespoons grated khoya/mawa

½ teaspoon Khazana garam masala powder (see annexure)

1 tablespoon chopped fresh mint leaves

2 teaspoons cornflour

½ teaspoon lemon juice

Butter for basting

2 teaspoons chaat masala (see annexure)

## Method

1.  Place the minced chicken in a mincer, add the ginger, garlic, green chillies, salt, one teaspoon green cardamom powder and white pepper powder and mince till smooth. Transfer into a bowl, add the ghee and mix well and keep it in a refrigerator for half an hour.

2.  In another bowl mix the paneer, khoya, half teaspoon green cardamom powder, garam masala powder, mint leaves, cornflour, lemon juice and salt. Keep it in the refrigerator for half an hour.

3.  Preheat an oven to 250ºC / 475ºF.

4.  Remove both the mixtures from the refrigerator and divide both of them into eight equal portions each.

5.  Pat on the paneer mixture onto skewers to form a cone tapering at both the ends.

6.  Pat on the chicken mixture over the paneer and press gently.

7.  Place the skewers on a baking tray and cook in the preheated oven for seven to eight minutes. Remove from the oven, baste with butter and cook for two to three minutes more.

8.  Remove the seekhs from the skewers, sprinkle with chaat masala and serve hot.

# Lal Murgh

This fried chicken is a little spicy. The presentation is spectacular – it comes hidden under the mound of shiny red button chillies... awesome! These button chillies, or boria chillies as they are also known, are small, round, hot peppers prized for the burning sensation that they produce in the mouth when bitten.

## Ingredients

400 grams boneless chicken, cut into 1 inch pieces

2 teaspoons garlic paste

1 teaspoon ginger paste

Salt to taste

1 tablespoon lemon juice

2 tablespoons red chilli paste

1 teaspoon crushed black peppercorns

1 teaspoon Khazana garam masala powder (see annexure)

1 egg, beaten

4 tablespoons refined flour (maida)

2 cups cornflakes, crushed

1 cup breadcrumbs

1 tablespoon oil + for deep frying

20 garlic cloves, chopped

2 teaspoons Kashmiri red chilli paste

1 cup red button (boria) chillies

1 teaspoon honey

1 teaspoon lemon juice

## Method

1. Mix together the chicken pieces, garlic paste, ginger paste, salt, lemon juice, red chilli paste, crushed peppercorns and garam masala powder and set aside in a refrigerator to marinate for one hour.

2. Heat sufficient oil in a kadai.

3. Add the egg and refined flour to the chicken and mix.

4. Put the crushed cornflakes and breadcrumbs in a bowl and mix.

5. Roll the chicken pieces in the cornflakes-breadcrumbs mixture and press between your palms to shape them into rounds. Deep fry in hot oil on medium heat till golden. Drain on absorbent paper.

6. Heat one tablespoon oil in a non stick wok, add garlic and sauté till brown. Add the red chilli paste and sauté for half a minute.

7. Add the chicken pieces and salt and toss well. Add the button chillies and toss well. Take the pan off the heat and add honey and lemon juice and toss.

8. Serve hot.

# Chandi Kaliyan

Translated, this one means 'buds of silver', enticing in the name itself. And in this dish the chicken cooked in a mild marinade is tender, epitomising the softness of a flower bud. Served decorated with silver foil, the grand presentation always impresses, making this a popular item at our restaurants. At a trial run, after some patrons suggested it was too bland, we did add some green chilli paste. But we soon found that our foreign guests were complaining that it was too spicy. So we went back to the original recipe.

## Ingredients

400 grams boneless chicken leg, cut into 16 pieces

2 teaspoons garlic paste

1 teaspoon ginger paste

Salt to taste

3½ teaspoons lemon juice

1¾ teaspoons white pepper powder

1 cup grated processed cheese

¾ cup fresh cream

½ cup hung yogurt

1 teaspoon green cardamom powder

A large of pinch nutmeg powder

Butter for basting

1 teaspoon chaat masala (see annexure)

1 sheet silver warq

## Method

1. Mix together the garlic paste, ginger paste, salt, one and half teaspoons lemon juice and three fourth teaspoon white pepper powder in a bowl. Add chicken pieces and mix well and set aside in a refrigerator to marinate for half an hour.

2. Mix together cheese, cream and hung yogurt in another bowl. Add green cardamom powder, nutmeg powder, one teaspoon white pepper powder and salt and mix well. Add the marinated chicken pieces and mix well. Set aside in the refrigerator to marinate for an hour longer.

3. Preheat oven to 250°C / 475°F.

4. String the chicken pieces onto skewers and cook in the preheated oven for ten minutes. Remove from the oven, baste with butter and cook for ten minutes longer.

5. Remove the chicken from the skewers and arrange on a plate. Sprinkle with chaat masala and remaining lemon juice, cover with silver warq and serve hot.

# Fish Amritsari

## Ingredients

275 grams boneless rawas, cut into 1½ inch pieces

2 tablespoons garlic paste

1 tablespoon ginger paste

½ tablespoon carom seeds (ajwain)

Salt to taste

1 teaspoon turmeric powder

1½ tablespoons Kashmiri red chilli paste

1 teaspoon Khazana garam masala powder (see annexure)

1 teaspoon vinegar

1½ tablespoons coriander powder

1 egg

1 tablespoon refined flour (maida)

4 tablespoons gram flour (besan)

Oil for deep frying

1 tablespoon chaat masala (see annexure)

½ tablespoon Kashmiri red chilli powder

½ tablespoon dried fenugreek leaves (kasoori methi)

The food of Punjab is to die for, popular with visitors and local residents alike. Batter fried batons of boneless fish – ever so succulent and melt in the mouth. A final sprinkle of kasoori methi gives this one that special zing.  It is easy to prepare and you will want to make it every other day. And we have been told by those who have eaten them at their place of origin - Amritsar - that ours is a better version!

## Method

1. Combine the garlic paste, ginger paste, carom seeds, salt, turmeric powder, red chilli paste and garam masala powder in a bowl.  Add fish and vinegar and mix well.

2. Add half tablespoon coriander powder, egg and refined flour and mix again.  Add gram flour and mix well.

3. Heat sufficient oil in a kadai and deep fry the fish on medium heat, till golden brown. Drain on absorbent paper.

4. Mix chaat masala, the remaining coriander powder, red chilli powder and kasoori methi and sprinkle the mixture on the fried fish.

5. Serve hot.

# Murgh Par Lutf

'Lutf' in Urdu means 'enjoyment' and this delicate kabab helps you to do just that – enjoy. Deliciously marinated in a rich and creamy mixture and cooked to golden perfection in the oven....absolute manna! Yogurt and cheese work towards not only tenderising the meat, but also add a special taste to the dish being made by providing a layer of fat that bastes the food as it cooks.

## Ingredients

400 grams boneless chicken breast, cut into 16 pieces

1 teaspoon chaat masala (see annexure)

2 teaspoons lemon juice

**For first marinade**

2 teaspoons lemon juice

Salt to taste

2 teaspoons garlic paste

1 teaspoon ginger paste

1 teaspoon green chilli paste

1 green chilli, chopped

1 teaspoon white pepper powder

**For second marinade**

½ cup grated processed cheese

½ cup fresh cream

½ cup hung yogurt

½ tablespoon oil

¼ teaspoon turmeric powder

1 teaspoon green cardamom powder

A pinch nutmeg powder

1 teaspoon white pepper powder

Salt to taste

2 teaspoons green chilli paste

2 tablespoons chopped fresh coriander leaves

½ green chilli, chopped

A large pinch of saffron soaked in 2 tablespoons warm milk

1 teaspoon cornflour

For basting

1 egg, beaten

1 tablespoon chopped fresh coriander leaves

1 teaspoon caraway seeds (shahi jeera)

⅓ cup grated processed cheese

½ tablespoon cornflour

## Method

1.  Mix the lemon juice, salt, garlic paste, ginger paste, green chilli paste, green chilli, white pepper powder and chicken pieces in a bowl and set aside in a refrigerator to marinate for half an hour.

2.  To make the second marinade, mix together in another bowl the cheese, cream and yogurt till smooth.

3.  Heat the oil in a small non stick pan, add turmeric powder and mix well. Add it to the cheese mixture along with green cardamom powder, nutmeg powder, white pepper powder, salt, green chilli paste, coriander leaves, green chilli, saffron milk and cornflour and mix well.

4.  Add the chicken pieces and mix well. Set aside to marinate in the refrigerator for half an hour more.

5.  Preheat an oven to 250°C / 475°F.

6.  String the chicken pieces onto skewers and cook in the preheated oven for ten minutes.

7.  Meanwhile beat the egg in another bowl, add coriander leaves, caraway seeds, cheese and cornflour and mix well for basting.

8.  Remove the chicken pieces from the oven, drizzle the egg mixture over them and return to the oven to cook for ten minutes more.

9.  Serve hot sprinkled with the chaat masala and lemon juice.

# Tandoori Prawns

Prawns are perhaps the most popular seafood that gets ordered the most in any restaurant. They are truly delicious, tender morsels of yumminess that get cooked very fast. Overcooking can spoil the texture as the prawns tend to become tough. Fresh catch cooked in the oven brings out the excellent flavour of the marinade. The best way to enjoy this is with lots of lemon juice and crunchy onion rings.

## Ingredients

16 jumbo prawns, shelled and deveined

For first marinade

1 tablespoon ginger paste

2 tablespoons garlic paste

1 tablespoon lemon juice

Salt to taste

For second marinade

1½ tablespoons oil

1 teaspoon turmeric powder

2 teaspoons Kashmiri red chilli powder

1 teaspoon Khazana garam masala powder     (see annexure)

1 tablespoon roasted gram flour (besan)

1 cup hung yogurt

1 teaspoon ginger paste

1 teaspoon garlic paste

Salt to taste

For garnish

1 large onion, cut into rings

1 lemon, cut into wedges

1 sprig fresh coriander leaves

## Method

1. For the first marinade, mix together the ginger paste, garlic paste, lemon juice and salt and apply it liberally on the prawns. Keep them aside for half an hour, preferably in a refrigerator.

2. Heat the oil in a non stick pan. Remove the pan from the heat and add the turmeric powder, Kashmiri red chilli powder, garam masala powder and roasted gram flour and mix well. Add this mixture to the yogurt and mix well.

3. Add the ginger paste, garlic paste and salt and mix well. Add the marinated prawns and mix well so that all the prawns are well coated. Set aside for half an hour, preferably in a refrigerator.

4. Preheat oven to 250°C / 475°F.

5. Arrange the prawns on a baking tray and bake in the preheated oven for eight to ten minutes.

6. Served hot with onion rings, lemon wedges and a sprig of fresh coriander leaves.

# Patiala Seekh

Tender lamb mince enriched with almonds and fresh spices, flavoured with our very own special garam masala and grilled – absolutely melts in the mouth!

## Ingredients

400 grams minced lamb (keema)

¼ cup browned onions

15 garlic cloves, chopped

1½ inch ginger piece, chopped

4 green chillies, finely chopped

1 small onion, sliced

40 grams lamb fat

¼ cup chopped fresh coriander leaves

2 tablespoons coarsely powdered cashewnuts

½ tablespoon crushed black peppercorns

Salt to taste

½ tablespoon coriander powder

½ tablespoon red chilli powder

½ tablespoon Khazana garam masala powder (see annexure)

½ egg, whisked

12 almonds, chopped

2 tablespoons butter

1 tablespoon roasted chana powder

To serve

Green chutney, as required (see annexure)

## Method

1. Preheat oven to 180°C/ 360°F.

2. Mince together the minced lamb, browned onions, garlic, ginger, green chillies, onion, lamb fat, coriander leaves, cashewnuts, peppercorns, salt, coriander powder, red chilli powder, garam masala powder, egg, almonds and butter in a mincer till smooth.

3. Transfer into a bowl, add the roasted chana powder and mix well.

4. Divide into eight equal portions and pat each portion onto a skewer to make seekhs.

5. Arrange the seekhs on a baking tray and cook in the preheated oven for eight to ten minutes or till cooked and golden.

6. Serve hot with green chutney.

# Vegetarian Main Course

# Vegetarian Main Course

# Dakhni Lasooni Palak

Yes indeed, this is a typically South Indian dish - quick cooked spinach with garlic, coconut and loads of curry leaves. You cannot stop at one helping...

## Ingredients

20-25 garlic cloves, chopped

2 medium bunches (700 grams) fresh spinach leaves, blanched and drained

3 teaspoons oil

1 tablespoon cumin seeds

1 tablespoon mustard seeds

1 medium onion, chopped

4 dried red chillies

20-25 curry leaves

¼ teaspoon asafoetida

⅔ cup scraped coconut + 1 tablespoon for garnishing

½ teaspoon turmeric powder

2 teaspoons coriander powder

⅓ cup butter

Salt to taste

1 tablespoon lemon juice

1 teaspoon dried mango powder (amchur)

2 tablespoons fried garlic (see recipe of Lasooni Naan)

## Method

1.  Chop half the blanched spinach leaves and make a puree of the rest.

2.  Heat the oil in a non stick pan, add the cumin seeds, mustard seeds and onion and sauté till lightly browned. Add the garlic, red chillies, curry leaves, asafoetida and one third cup scraped coconut and sauté till fragrant.

3.  Add the turmeric powder and coriander powder and sauté for a minute. Add the chopped spinach and sauté for five minutes on medium heat.

4.  Add the butter and continue to sauté. Add the spinach puree and sauté till dry. Add the salt and mix well.

5.  Add the lemon juice and dried mango powder and mix. Add the remaining scraped coconut and mix.

6.  Transfer the spinach into a serving bowl and serve hot, garnished with one tablespoon scraped coconut and fried garlic.

# Aloo Bukhara Kofta

Apricots are often used in Indian cuisine not just for the taste of the fruit – fresh during the short season, or dried all through the year – but for its many health benefits. This dish is the perfect example of a blend of Punjabi, North West Frontier and Kashmiri cuisines – nut-stuffed dried plums, their sweetness ensconced in feather-light paneer and khoya koftas and served with a flavourful yellow gravy. An innovative avatar of the malai kofta, this one is placed high on the patrons' list.

## Ingredients

### For koftas

8 apricots, soaked and stoned

1½ cups grated cottage cheese (paneer)

¾ cup + 1 teaspoon grated khoya/ mawa

1 medium potato, boiled, peeled and mashed

⅔ cup + 2 tablespoons cornflour

Salt to taste

½ teaspoon green cardamom powder

2 green chillies, finely chopped

1½ inch ginger, cut into thin strips and soaked in 2 tablespoons lemon juice

1 tablespoon raisins (kishmish)

1 tablespoon roasted and crushed cashewnuts

Oil for deep frying

### For gravy

⅓ cup oil

1 black cardamom

7 green cardamoms

3½-inch cinnamon sticks

1 large onion, sliced

2 teaspoons ginger paste

2 teaspoons garlic paste

2 teaspoons caraway seeds (shahi jeera)

⅔ cup broken cashewnuts

⅔ cup melon seeds (magaz)

⅓ cup tomato puree

1 teaspoon turmeric powder

2 teaspoons coriander powder

4 teaspoons green chilli paste

⅔ cup yogurt

⅔ teaspoon sugar

⅓ cup khoya / mawa

2⅔ tablespoons coconut milk powder

2 teaspoons screw pine (kewda) water

2 teaspoons rose water

### For garnish

1 teaspoon fresh cream

1 sprig fresh coriander leaves

## Method

1.  For the koftas, mix together the paneer, three fourth cup khoya and potato in a bowl and knead till smooth. Add the cornflour, salt and green cardamom powder and knead again.

2.  For stuffing, mix the green chillies, ginger, raisins, cashewnuts and one teaspoon khoya. Stuff this mixture into the apricots.

3.  Heat sufficient oil in a kadai.

4.  Divide the paneer mixture into eight portions and stuff each portion with a stuffed apricot and roll again, ensuring that the apricots are completely covered with the paneer mixture.

5.  Deep fry these koftas on medium heat, stirring gently, till light brown. Drain on absorbent paper.

6.  For the gravy, heat the oil in a deep non stick pan. Add the

black cardamom, green cardamoms and cinnamon and sauté for two minutes. Add the onion and sauté for two minutes. Add the ginger paste and garlic paste and sauté for two to three minutes or till well browned.

7. Add the caraway seeds and sauté for ten seconds. Add the cashewnuts and melon seeds and sauté till the oil separates.

8. Add the tomato puree and sauté for five minutes. Add the turmeric powder, coriander powder and green chilli paste and sauté for a minute.

9. Add the yogurt and mix well. Add one and a half cups water and mix well and let the gravy come to a boil. Take the pan off the heat and let it cool.

10. Strain and grind the residue to a fine puree. Transfer it back into the pan and add the strained stock. Add the sugar and khoya and mix well. Mix the coconut milk powder in one third cup water and add to the gravy. Add the kewda and rose waters and mix. Bring the gravy to a boil.

11. To serve, arrange the koftas in a serving bowl, pour the gravy over them. Garnish with fresh cream and coriander sprigs and serve hot.

# Bharwan Bhindi Do Pyaza

As the name suggests, this dish has onion dominating the overall flavour. A superbly crafted dish that glorifies the humble bhindi, you would enjoy making it a Sunday special at home.

## Ingredients

500 grams ladyfingers (bhindi)

Oil for deep frying

### For stuffing

1 tablespoon oil

4 dried red chillies

3 tablespoons coriander seeds

1 tablespoon cumin seeds

1 tablespoon white sesame seeds (safed til)

5 cloves

2 black cardamoms

2 one-inch cinnamon sticks

1 tablespoon black peppercorns

2 tablespoons stone flower (dagad phool)

7 bay leaves

### For gravy

2 tablespoons oil

1 tablespoon cumin seeds

5 crushed green cardamoms

1 tablespoon crushed coriander seeds

2 medium onions, sliced

1 tablespoon garlic paste

1 tablespoon ginger paste

1 medium tomato, chopped

½ teaspoon turmeric powder

1 teaspoon red chilli powder

2 teaspoons coriander powder

1 teaspoon cumin powder

Salt to taste

½ cup yogurt, whisked

16 sambhar onions

½ cup browned onions

1 inch ginger piece, cut into thin strips

¼ cup chopped fresh coriander leaves

½ tablespoon chaat masala (see annexure)

### For garnish

½ teaspoon pickled ginger strips (see note below)

1 tablespoon chopped fresh coriander leaves

## Method

1. To make the stuffing, heat the oil in a non stick pan, add the red chillies, coriander seeds, cumin seeds, sesame seeds, cloves, black cardamoms, cinnamon, black peppercorns, stone flower and bay leaves and sauté on medium heat till fragrant. Cool and grind into a coarse powder.

2. Heat sufficient oil in a kadai.

3. Trim the heads of the ladyfingers and make a slit in the middle of each, leaving quarter inch at either end. Stuff each one with the spice powder.

4. Deep fry the ladyfingers in hot oil on medium heat till golden and crisp. Drain on absorbent paper and set aside.

5. For the gravy, heat the oil in a non stick pan, add the cumin seeds, green cardamoms, coriander seeds, onions, garlic paste and ginger paste and sauté till the onions are well browned.

6. Add quarter cup water and the tomato and sauté till tomato softens. Add the turmeric powder, red chilli powder, coriander powder and cumin powder and sauté for five minutes. Add the salt and yogurt and mix well.

7. Add the sambhar onions and sauté for five minutes. Add half cup water and mix. Cook till all the moisture evaporates.

8. Add the browned onions, fried ladyfingers, ginger strips, coriander leaves and chaat masala and cook for two minutes.

9. Serve hot, garnished with pickled ginger strips and coriander leaves.

## Note

To make pickled ginger strips, cut ginger into thin strips and soak in lemon juice.

# Makhanwala Paneer

This dish is a hot favourite in North India, where milk and milk products are in plentiful supply. Soft paneer cubes drenched in makhni gravy redolent with spice and all things nice…. Just go for it with naan or roti. Eaten with hot flaky paranthas or crisp naan, it is a treat for the senses and the stomach.

## Ingredients

400 grams cottage cheese (paneer), cut into 1 inch cubes

500 grams tomatoes, quartered

7-8 garlic cloves

1½ inch ginger piece, roughly chopped

7 green cardamoms

½ blade mace

2 tablespoons red chilli (deghi mirch) powder

½ cup butter

Salt to taste

1½ teaspoons dried fenugreek leaves (kasoori methi) powder

1 tablespoon honey

¼ cup fresh cream

1 teaspoon Khazana garam masala powder (see annexure)

For garnish

2 teaspoons fresh cream

1 sprig fresh coriander leaves

## Method

1. Heat a deep non stick pan. Add the tomatoes, garlic, ginger, green cardamoms, mace, one cup water, red chilli powder and butter and let it boil for fifteen minutes.

2. Add the salt and mix well.  Take the pan off the heat and allow it to cool.

3. Blend the gravy to a fine puree, strain into another deep non stick pan and cook for five minutes.

4. Add the paneer cubes, kasoori methi powder and honey and cook for further two to three minutes. Add the cream and garam masala powder and mix lightly.

5. Transfer into a serving dish, garnish with a swirl of fresh cream and a coriander sprig and serve hot.

# Malai Kofta

## Ingredients

1 medium potato, boiled, peeled and grated

100 grams grated cottage cheese (paneer)

100 gram grated khoya/mawa

1 teaspoon green cardamom powder

Salt to taste

1 teaspoon white pepper powder

1 green chilli, chopped

¼ cup chopped fresh coriander leaves + a sprig for garnishing

4 tablespoons cornflour

Oil for deep frying

1 sheet silver foil (chaandi ka warq)

For the gravy

¼ cup oil

7 crushed green cardamoms

2 one-inch crushed cinnamon sticks

2 crushed black cardamoms

4 crushed cloves

1 cup boiled onion paste

½ cup grated khoya/mawa

¼ cup scraped coconut

¾ cup kaju-magaz paste (see annexure)

Salt to taste

½ teaspoon white pepper powder

2 teaspoons green chilli paste

1 teaspoon green cardamom powder

2 tablespoons ghee

2 teaspoons chopped fresh coriander leaves

This definitely is a dish for those special occasions. There are quite a few versions of this, but this one is my favourite. It is a vegetarian alternative to mutton koftas and goes excellently with both naans, rotis or even with jeera rice.

## Method

1. Heat sufficient oil in a kadai.

2. In a bowl mix together potato, paneerand khoya well. Add green cardamom powder, salt, white pepper powder, green chilli, coriander leaves and cornflour and mix well.

3. Divide the mixture into eight equal portions and shape them into balls.

4. Deep fry in hot oil on medium heat till light golden in colour. Drain on absorbent paper and set aside.

5. For the gravy heat the oil in a deep non stick pan. Add green cardamoms, cinnamon, black cardamoms and cloves and sauté till fragrant. Add boiled onion paste and sauté for five minutes on low heat.

6. Add khoya and coconut and sauté for two to three minutes. Add kaju-magaz paste and salt and mix well.

7. Add four cups water, white pepper powder, green chilli paste, green cardamom powder and bring the gravy to a boil. Add ghee and mix well.

8. Strain the gravy into another non stick pan and grind the residue. Add the residue to the strained gravy and mix well. Add coriander leaves and mix well and bring it to a boil and cook for two to three minutes.

9. Transfer the gravy into a serving bowl, halve the koftas and place them over the gravy.

10. Serve hot garnished with chaandikawarq and a sprig of coriander leaves.

# Kadai Tandoori Gobhi Mussallam

Another visual treat – whole cauliflower, marinated and cooked in an oven or tandoor, laced with rich and highly aromatic gravy. Absolutely the ultimate!

## Ingredients

400 grams cauliflower

2 tablespoons oil

1 cup hung yogurt

1 teaspoon turmeric powder

1½ teaspoons Kashmiri red chilli powder

1½ teaspoons Khazana garam masala powder (see annexure)

2 tablespoons roasted gram flour (besan)

Salt to taste

1 teaspoon dried fenugreek leaves (kasoori methi)

**For gravy**

2 medium onions

3 tablespoons oil

½ tablespoon ginger paste

½ tablespoon garlic paste

1 tablespoon mussallam masala (see annexure)

1 large pinch turmeric powder

1 teaspoon coriander powder

¼ cup kaju-magaz paste (see annexure)

¼ cup yogurt, whisked

1 teaspoon red chilli powder

¼ cup browned onion paste

Salt to taste

7-8 garlic cloves, chopped

¼ tablespoon kadai masala (see annexure)

1 medium green capsicum, diced

1 medium tomato, diced

½ cup chopped fresh coriander leaves

1 sheet silver warq

## Method

1. Remove the leaves and blanch the whole cauliflower in boiling water for eight to ten minutes. Drain and set aside.

2. Heat the oil in a non stick pan. Take the pan off the heat and add the turmeric powder, red chilli powder, garam masala powder and gram flour and mix thoroughly. Add this to the hung yogurt along with salt and kasoori methi and mix till smooth. Marinate the blanched cauliflower in this for thirty minutes.

3. Preheat oven to 250°C/475°F.

4. Place the cauliflower on a baking tray and bake in the preheated oven for twenty five minutes.

5. For the gravy, slice one onion and dice the other.

6. Heat two tablespoons oil in a non stick kadai. Add the sliced onion and sauté till brown. Add the ginger and garlic pastes and sauté for two minutes. Add the mussallam masala and sauté for half a minute.

7. Add the turmeric powder, coriander powder and kaju-magaz paste and mix well. Add the yogurt and red chilli powder and mix well.

8. Add the browned onion paste and mix. Sauté for five minutes. Add the salt and three fourth cup water and mix well. Simmer for a minute and strain the gravy into another non stick pan.

9. Heat the remaining oil in another non stick pan, add the chopped garlic and kadai masala and sauté till fragrant.

10. Add the diced onion, capsicum, tomato and the strained gravy and sauté for two minutes.

11. Add the coriander leaves and mix well. Take the pan off the heat.

12. To serve, place the baked cauliflower in the centre of a serving bowl and cut it into eight pieces. Pour the gravy over, decorate with silver warq and serve hot.

# Note

To make browned onion paste slice 2 large onions and deep fry till well browned. This will give 1 cup browned onions. Cool and grind with yogurt in the ratio of 1:1 - i.e. one cup browned onions with one cup yogurt.

# Dhingri Matar Hara Pyaaz

Dhingri or mushrooms are an excellent vegetarian substitute in a lot of non-vegetarian dishes. But in this dish, the mushroom is king. Combined with green peas and spring onions…it cannot get any tastier!

## Ingredients

22 button mushrooms, blanched and halved

1 cup green peas, boiled

¼ cup oil

1 tablespoon cumin seeds

1 cup chopped spring onion bulbs

2 medium tomatoes, chopped

½ teaspoon turmeric powder

1 tablespoon coriander powder

1 tablespoon Kashmiri red chilli powder

1 teaspoon Khazana garam masala powder (see annexure)

Salt to taste

½ cup kaju-magaz paste (see annexure)

2 tablespoons dried fenugreek leaves (kasoori methi)

1½ cups chopped spring onion greens

1 tablespoon chaat masala

1 stalk of spring onion greens, diagonally sliced

## Method

1. Heat the oil in a non stick kadai and add the cumin seeds. When they begin to change colour, add the spring onion bulbs and sauté till well browned.

2. Add the tomatoes and sauté till the oil surfaces. Add the turmeric powder, coriander powder, red chilli powder and garam masala powder and continue to sauté. Add the salt and sauté for five minutes.

3. Add the kaju-magaz paste and mix well. Add the mushrooms and peas and mix well.

4. Add one and half cups water, kasoori methi and spring onion greens and mix. Cook for five minutes.

5. Add the chaat masala and mix.

6. Serve hot garnished with spring onion greens.

# Makai Baingan Bharta

Bharta can be made from a number of vegetables, but roasted or charred brinjal or baingan, is perhaps the most popular in India. Garlic adds an extra punch to the flavourful onion-tomato masala in which roasted brinjal and corn is served…breathe in the aroma as it comes piping hot to the table.

## Ingredients

1 cup corn kernels (makai), boiled

1 large (450 grams) brinjal

25-20 garlic cloves, chopped

4 tablespoons ghee

1 tablespoon cumin seeds

1 tablespoon onion seeds (kalonji)

2 medium onions, chopped

Salt to taste

1½ inch ginger piece, chopped

1 medium tomato, chopped

5 green chillies, chopped

2 teaspoons red chilli powder

1 teaspoon turmeric powder

1 tablespoon coriander powder

2 teaspoons cumin powder

2 teaspoons dried mango powder (amchur)

2 teaspoons chaat masala (see annexure)

¼ cup + 2 tablespoons chopped fresh coriander leaves

1 tablespoon lemon juice

## Method

1. Pierce one garlic clove into the brinjal and roast it over open flame till the skin is charred and peels off. This may take about fifteen minutes. Set aside to cool.

2. Chop the remaining garlic. When cooled, remove the skin of the brinjal and mash the pulp well.

3. Heat the ghee in a non stick kadai and add the cumin seeds and onion seeds. Cook on medium heat for half a minute. Add the onions and salt and sauté till light brown.

4. Add the garlic and ginger and sauté for a minute. Add the tomato and green chillies and sauté for four minutes. Add one cup water and cook for two to three minutes.

5. Add the red chilli powder, turmeric powder, coriander powder, cumin powder, dried mango powder and chaat masala and mix well. Cook for two to three minutes.

6. Add the corn and mashed brinjal and half a cup of water. Mix and cook for three to four minutes.

7. Add a quarter cup of coriander leaves and take the pan off the heat. Add the lemon juice and mix. Serve hot, garnished with the remaining coriander leaves.

# Methi Aloo Mangodi

Fried moong wadis add crunch and a unique texture to a mix of fresh fenugreek and baby potatoes. And the garlic flavoured masala raises the dish to unexpected heights.

## Ingredients

100 grams fresh fenugreek leaves (use only leaves)

350 grams baby potatoes, boiled and peeled

1 cup mangodi (green gram dumplings)

¼ cup oil + for deep frying

1 tablespoon cumin seeds

½ teaspoon asafoetida

4 dried red chillies

2 medium onions, chopped

Salt to taste

30 garlic cloves, chopped

1½ inch ginger, chopped

2 medium tomatoes, chopped

1 teaspoon Kashmiri red chilli powder

1 teaspoon turmeric powder

2 teaspoons coriander powder

1 teaspoon cumin powder

1 cup yogurt

1 tablespoon chopped fresh coriander leaves

## Method

1. Heat sufficient oil in a kadai and deep fry the mangodi till light golden. Drain and soak in two cups of water for fifteen minutes.

2. Blanch the fenugreek leaves in boiling water for two to three minutes. Drain well and squeeze out excess water. Chop.

3. Heat quarter cup oil in a non stick kadai and add cumin seeds. When they begin to change colour, add the asafoetida, red chillies and sauté for three minutes.

4. Add the onions and sauté till they are lightly browned. Add the salt, garlic and ginger and mix well.

5. Add the tomatoes and cook till they turn pulpy. Add the fenugreek leaves and cook for two to three minutes.

6. Add the red chilli powder, turmeric powder, coriander powder, cumin powder and potatoes and mix well.

7. Add the mangodi and mix. Cook for two to three minutes. Add the yogurt and let the gravy come to a boil.

8. Serve hot, garnished with coriander leaves.

# Reshmi Paneer

A colourful medley of silky smooth paneer strips stir fried with mildly spiced tomato, three coloured capsicums and onion. A treat indeed, both for the eyes and the palate.

## Ingredients

500 grams cottage cheese (paneer), cut into 1 inch batons

½ cup + 1 tablespoon oil

4 black cardamoms

20 green cardamoms

2 one-inch cinnamon sticks

4 medium onions, sliced

1 tablespoon ginger paste

2 tablespoons garlic paste

1 tablespoon cumin seeds

½ cup cashewnuts

½ cup melon seeds (magaz)

1 cup tomato puree

1 cup yogurt, whisked

2 tablespoons coriander powder

1 tablespoon turmeric powder

¼ cup green chilli paste

4 tablespoon butter

1 tablespoon Khazana garam masala powder (see annexure)

½ cup khoya/ mawa

2 medium onions, thickly sliced and layers separated

1 medium green capsicum, cut into 1½ inch batons

1 medium red capsicum, cut into 1½ inch batons

1 medium yellow capsicum, cut into 1½ inch batons

2 medium tomatoes, halved, seeded and cut into 1½ inch batons

½ cup + 2 teaspoons fresh cream

½ tablespoon green cardamom powder

¼ cup chopped fresh coriander leaves

## Method

1. Heat half cup oil in a non stick pan, add the black cardamoms, green cardamoms and cinnamon and sauté till fragrant.

2. Add the onions and sauté till browned. Add the ginger paste and one tablespoon garlic paste and sauté for a minute.

3. Add the cumin seeds, cashewnuts and melon seeds and sauté for a minute.

4. Add the tomato puree, yogurt, coriander powder, turmeric powder, green chilli paste and butter and mix well.

5. Add the garam masala powder and khoya and mix well. Add one and a half cups water and mix. Let the gravy come to a boil. Switch off the heat and let the mixture cool.

6. Strain off excess liquid and grind the residue. Transfer into a bowl and add the strained liquid and mix.

7. Heat one tablespoon oil in deep non stick pan and add one tablespoon garlic paste and sauté.

8. Add the onions, green capsicum, red capsicum, yellow capsicum and tomatoes and mix. Add the gravy and cook for five minutes.

9. Add the paneer and mix gently.

10. Add half cup cream, green cardamom powder and coriander leaves and mix gently.

11. Transfer into a serving bowl, garnish with a swirl of cream and serve hot.

# Shaam Savera

Our signature preparation, the colours of this dish – saffron, white and green - proclaim our nationalism. Spinach koftas are filled with paneer and served floating on a saffron coloured, velvety gravy. It also stands for shaam, or dusk, as represented by the darker shades of the spinach, while the paleness of the paneer symbolizes savera or dawn. When displayed as koftas cut open in half to show off the light inside, the dish is more than just food, it is poetry on a plate.

## Ingredients

### For spinach covering

2 small bunches (500 grams) fresh spinach leaves, blanched, drained and pureed

2 tablespoons butter

1 tablespoon caraway seeds (shahi jeera)

5 garlic cloves, chopped

1 inch ginger piece, chopped

2 teaspoons green chilli paste

1 teaspoon green cardamom powder

1 teaspoon coriander powder

3 tablespoons cashewnut powder

Salt to taste

8 tablespoons roasted chana powder

Cornflour for dusting

### For kofta filling

½ cup grated cottage cheese (paneer)

¼ tablespoon green cardamom powder

¼ tablespoon white pepper powder

Salt to taste

¼ tablespoon cornflour

Oil for deep frying

### For gravy

¼ cup oil

½ teaspoon caraway seeds (shahi jeera)

2 cloves

2 black cardamoms

10 green cardamoms

1 inch cinnamon stick

1 medium onion, sliced

8 garlic cloves, chopped

1 inch piece ginger, chopped

1 teaspoon turmeric powder

5 medium tomatoes, halved

½ tablespoon red chilli (deghi mirch) powder

Salt to taste

⅓ cup butter

¼ cup broken cashewnuts

1½ tablespoons dried fenugreek leaves (kasoori methi)

½ tablespoon green cardamom powder

1 teaspoon honey

### For garnish

2 teaspoons fresh cream

½ ginger piece, cut into thin strips

1 green chilli, seeded and cut into thin strips

## Method

1. For the spinach covering, melt the butter in a non stick pan. Add the caraway seeds and sauté until they begin to change colour. Add the spinach puree, garlic, ginger, green chilli paste, green cardamom powder, coriander powder, cashewnut powder, salt and roasted chana powder and cook, stirring, till dry. Spread it out on a plate and set aside in a refrigerator to cool completely.

2. For the kofta filling, mix together the paneer, cardamom powder, white pepper powder, salt and cornflour and mix well.

3. Divide into eight equal portions and roll into balls. Keep them in the refrigerator till required.

4. For the gravy, heat the oil in a deep non stick pan. Add the caraway seeds, cloves, black cardamoms, green cardamoms, cinnamon, onion, garlic, ginger and turmeric powder and sauté for five to seven minutes.

5. Add the tomatoes, red chilli powder, salt and one cup water and cook, stirring for five minutes. Add the butter, cashewnuts, kasoori methi, green cardamom powder and honey and mix well. Let the gravy simmer for ten to fifteen minutes on medium heat. Set aside to cool.

6. Grind and strain the gravy into a bowl and discard the residue.

7. To make the koftas, heat sufficient oil in a kadai. Divide the spinach mixture into eight equal portions. Coat each paneer ball with a portion of spinach and roll into a round ball. Roll the balls lightly in cornflour. Deep fry on medium heat for three to four minutes. Drain on absorbent paper and set aside to cool slightly.

8. To serve, pour the curry into a serving bowl. Halve the koftas horizontally and place them on the top of the gravy.

9. Garnish with a swirl of fresh cream, ginger and green chilli strips and serve.

# Subz Panchmael

Sizzling vegetables in a kadai – baby corn, baby potatoes, capsicums, cauliflower, carrots and French beans in a rich and spicy gravy.

## Ingredients

10 baby corns, cut into diamonds and blanched

8 baby potatoes, peeled, halved and blanched

1½ medium green capsicums, cut into diamonds

1 medium carrot, cut into diamonds and blanched

⅛ cauliflower, separated into small florets and blanched

12-14 French beans, cut into diamonds and blanched

5 teaspoons oil

1 tablespoon cumin seeds

1 medium onion, chopped

20-25 garlic cloves, chopped

1½ inch ginger piece, chopped

Salt to taste

½ cup fresh tomato puree

½ teaspoon turmeric powder

1 teaspoon red chilli powder

2 teaspoons coriander powder

2 teaspoons cumin powder

½ cup kaju-magaz paste (see annexure)

¼ cup + 1 tablespoon chopped fresh coriander leaves

2 teaspoons chaat masala (see annexure)

1 tablespoon lemon juice

## Method

1.  Heat the oil in a non stick kadai, add the cumin seeds and onion and sauté till lightly browned. Add the garlic and ginger and sauté for two minutes.
2.  Add the salt and tomato puree and sauté till dry. Add the turmeric powder, red chilli powder, coriander powder, cumin powder and half cup of water. Mix and sauté till fragrant. Add the kaju-magaz paste and mix well.
3.  Add the baby corns, baby potatoes, green capsicums, carrot, cauliflower and French beans and sauté for two minutes. Add half cup water and mix.
4.  Add one fourth cup coriander leaves, chaat masala and lemon juice and mix well.
5.  Serve hot, garnished with the remaining coriander leaves.

# Tawa Aloo Jeera

## Ingredients

32 (approximately 550 grams) baby potatoes, boiled and peeled

2 teaspoons oil

1 tablespoon cumin seeds

1 small onion, chopped

1 small tomato, chopped

1 tablespoon Kashmiri red chilli powder

1 tablespoon coriander powder

1 tablespoon cumin powder

½ tablespoon turmeric powder

1 tablespoon chaat masala (see annexure)

Salt to taste

½ cup chopped fresh coriander leaves

Comfort food for many – the simple jeera aloo. But here we have raised it to another level with a few twists. Jeera or cumin is the second most popular spice all over the world, black pepper being the first, but in this dish it rules the roost.

## Method

1. Heat the oil on a non stick tawa, add the cumin seeds and sauté till they change colour.

2. Add the onion and sauté till lightly browned. Add the tomato and cook for five to six minutes on medium heat.

3. Add the red chilli powder, coriander powder, half cup water, cumin powder, turmeric powder and chaat masala and mix well. Sauté for two to three minutes.

4. Add the salt and potatoes and mix. Add half cup water and simmer for four to five minutes.

5. Add the coriander leaves and mix. Serve hot.

# Zannat-e-Numa

'Zannat-e-numa' means 'beautiful heaven', and that is where this dish takes you – to! The humble, everyday potato is given a delicious lift with a poetic name. Potato lovers will absolutely love the exotic stuffed spuds baked and served in a delightful green gravy. We've seen many a pleased smile on our guests' faces when this is brought to the table.

## Ingredients

5 large potatoes, peeled

Oil for deep frying

**For marinade**

1 tablespoon oil

½ teaspoon turmeric powder

2 tablespoons red chilli powder

¾ teaspoon Khazana garam masala powder (see annexure)

1 tablespoon roasted gram flour (besan)

½ cup hung yogurt

Salt to taste

½ teaspoon dried fenugreek leaves (kasoori methi)

¼ tablespoon ginger paste

½ tablespoon garlic paste

¼ teaspoon green chilli paste

**For stuffing**

½ cup grated cottage cheese (paneer)

¾ inch ginger piece, chopped

1 tablespoon chopped fresh coriander leaves

1 tablespoon chopped fresh mint leaves

10 raisins, chopped

6 fried and crushed cashewnuts

½ teaspoon red chilli powder

¾ teaspoon chaat masala (see annexure)

Salt to taste

½ teaspoon cumin powder

**For gravy**

2 tablespoons ghee

½ teaspoon caraway seeds (shahi jeera)

2 medium onions, chopped

¾ cup fresh tomato puree

10 garlic cloves, chopped

½ inch ginger piece, chopped

¼ cup kaju-magaz paste (see annexure)

1 pinch turmeric powder

1½ teaspoons Kashmiri red chilli powder

2½ teaspoons coriander powder

1½ teaspoons Khazana garam masala powder (see annexure)

Salt to taste

1 bunch (330 grams) fresh spinach leaves, blanched and pureed

3 tablespoons butter

1 teaspoon dried fenugreek leaves (kasoori methi)

½ cup yogurt, whisked

½ cup + 2 teaspoons fresh cream

½ teaspoon green cardamom powder

½ teaspoon lemon juice

**For garnish**

¼ teaspoon red chilli flakes

¼ teaspoon sesame (til) seeds

5-6 spinach leaves, cut into thin strips and deep fried

## Method

1.  Preheat oven to 250°C/ 475°F.

2.  Slice off a thin slice from the tops of four potatoes and scoop out the centre to give a barrel shape. Keep the trimmings aside. Halve the remaining potato. Blanch the potatoes in boiling water for ten minutes. Drain thoroughly.

3.  Heat sufficient oil in a kadai and deep fry the potato

barrels, one half of the fifth potato and the trimmings separately, till light golden. Drain on absorbent paper. Mash the trimmings and the half potato and set aside.

4. For the marinade, heat the oil in a non stick pan. Remove the pan from the heat and add the turmeric powder, red chilli powder, garam masala powder and roasted gram flour and mix well. Add this to the hung yogurt along with salt, kasoori methi, ginger paste, garlic paste and green chilli paste to make a smooth mixture.

5. For the stuffing, mix together the grated paneer, fried and mashed potato, ginger, coriander leaves, mint leaves, raisins, cashewnuts, red chilli powder, chaat masala, salt and cumin powder.

6. Stuff this mixture into the fried potatoes. Coat the potatoes with the marinade and arrange them upright on a baking tray. Bake them in the preheated oven for fifteen minutes.

7. For the gravy, heat the ghee in a non stick pan, add the caraway seeds and sauté for half a minute. Add onions and sauté till light brown.

8. Add the tomato puree, garlic and ginger and sauté till the oil surfaces. Add the kaju-magaz paste, turmeric powder, red chilli powder, two teaspoons coriander powder, one teaspoon garam masala powder and salt and sauté for five minutes.

9. Add the spinach puree and sauté for five minutes. Add the butter, kasoori methi and sauté for two minutes.

10. Add the yogurt and cook for five minutes. Add half cup water and half cup cream and cook for two to three minutes more.

11. Add the green cardamom powder, remaining garam masala powder, remaining coriander powder and lemon juice. Mix well and take the pan off the heat.

12. Pour the gravy into a serving bowl and arrange the potatoes on top of it. Serve hot garnished with a swirl of fresh cream, red chilli flakes, sesame seeds and fried spinach strips.

81

# Paneer Pudina Kalimirch

At most restaurants, paneer is hailed supreme in the vegetarian menu. Easy to make and easy to use it is versatile. It takes on any flavour easily and mingles with most gravies beautifully. Here it blends well with aromatic fresh mint and peppercorns. In fact, we have been told that this dish makes every visit to TYC worth it!

## Ingredients

400 grams cottage cheese (paneer), cut into ½ inch cubes

⅓ cup fresh mint paste

1⅓ teaspoons crushed black peppercorns

6½ teaspoons oil

1⅓ teaspoons cumin seeds

1 medium onion, chopped

Salt to taste

½ large tomato, chopped

⅔ teaspoon turmeric powder

1⅓ teaspoons coriander powder

⅔ teaspoon red chilli powder

⅔ tablespoon green chilli paste

⅓ bunch (110 grams) fresh spinach leaves, blanched and ground

½ cup cashewnut paste

1 tablespoon coriander paste

½ cup butter

⅔ teaspoon Khazana garam masala powder

1⅓ teaspoons dried mango powder (amchur)

1⅓ teaspoons chaat masala

⅔ tablespoon lemon juice

### For garnish

1 fresh mint sprig

½ teaspoon crushed black peppercorns

## Method

1. Heat the oil in a non stick kadai and add cumin seeds. When they begin to change colour, add the crushed black peppercorns and onion and sauté till the onion is browned.

2. Add the salt and tomato and sauté till soft.

3. Add the turmeric powder, coriander powder and red chilli powder and mix well. Add the mint paste and green chilli paste and cook till the raw flavours disappear.

4. Add the spinach and cook till the raw flavours disappear. Add the cashewnut paste and mix well and cook for four to five minutes.

5. Add two cups of water and mix well and cook till dry.

6. Add the coriander paste, butter, garam masala powder, dried mango powder and chaat masala and mix well. Add the paneer cubes and mix gently. Simmer for two minutes.

7. Add the lemon juice and mix well.

8. Garnish with the mint sprig and crushed black peppercorns and serve hot.

# Non-vegetarian Main Course

# Non-vegetarian Main Course

# Bhuna Gosht

## Ingredients

750 grams mutton on bone, cut into 1½ inch pieces

6 green cardamoms

10-12 black peppercorns

5-6 cloves

2 dried red chillies

⅓ cup oil

7 large onions, chopped

2 tablespoons garlic paste

1 tablespoon ginger paste

1 tablespoon red chilli powder

¼ teaspoon turmeric powder

1¼ tablespoons coriander powder

¼ teaspoon green cardamom powder

Salt to taste

1 cup yogurt, whisked

3 large tomatoes, chopped

2 tablespoons chopped fresh coriander leaves

1 inch ginger, cut into thin strips

Bhuna means sautéed and that's what gives this mutton dish that special flavor. A favourite of our patrons, it's one of the fastest moving items on our menu. While buying the mutton see to it that it is of a young lamb, for then the meat will be tender and will withstand all that sautéing.

## Method

1. Coarsely crush the green cardamoms, black peppercorns, cloves and dry red chillies.

2. Heat oil in a non-stick pan. Add the crushed spices and sauté for half a minute. Add onions and cook until brown.

3. Add garlic paste and ginger paste and sauté for a minute.

4. Add mutton pieces and sauté till light brown. Add red chilli powder, turmeric powder, coriander powder, green cardamom powder and salt and mix well.

5. Add yogurt and mix well. Cover and cook on low heat for thirty to thirty-five minutes.

6. Add tomatoes, mix well, cover and cook on low heat for half an hour or till mutton is tender.

7. Serve hot garnished with coriander leaves and ginger strips.

# Chaandi Korma

Much of the food that is classed as 'Moghlai' is rich and high in calories. But the flavours of the gravies and the tenderness of the meats in the dishes make them so very delicious, that you tend to not just eat but over-eat! The richness is made even more appetising with the use of varq, or silver foil. A regal sight that can pretty up many a party table.

## Ingredients

400 grams boneless chicken leg, cut into 16 pieces

2 teaspoons garlic paste

1 teaspoon ginger paste

Salt to taste

3½ teaspoons lemon juice

1¾ teaspoons white pepper powder

1 cup grated processed cheese

¾ cup fresh cream

½ cup hung yogurt

1 teaspoon green cardamom powder

A large pinch nutmeg powder

1 teaspoon chaat masala (see annexure)

Butter for basting

1 sheet silver warq

1 sprig fresh mint leaves

**For gravy**

¼ cup oil

7 crushed green cardamoms

2 crushed black cardamoms

2 one-inch crushed cinnamon sticks

4 crushed cloves

1 cup boiled onion paste

½ cup grated khoya/mawa

¾ cup kaju-magaz paste (see annexure)

Salt to taste

½ teaspoon white pepper powder

2 teaspoons green chilli paste

1 teaspoon green cardamom powder

2 tablespoons ghee

2 teaspoons mint powder

2 inch ginger piece, cut into thin strips

¼ cup fresh cream

## Method

1.  Mix together the garlic paste, ginger paste, salt, one and half teaspoons lemon juice and three fourth teaspoon white pepper powder in a bowl. Add chicken pieces and mix well and set aside in a refrigerator to marinate for half an hour.

2.  Mix together the cheese, cream and hung yogurt in another bowl. Add the green cardamom powder, nutmeg powder, one teaspoon white pepper powder and salt and mix well. Add the marinated chicken pieces and mix well. Set aside in a refrigerator to marinate for an hour more.

3.  Preheat oven to 250°C / 475°F.

4.  String the chicken pieces onto skewers and cook in the preheated oven for ten minutes. Remove from the oven, baste with butter and cook for ten minutes more. Remove the chicken from the skewers and arrange on a plate. Sprinkle with chaat masala and lemon juice and set aside.

5.  For the gravy, heat the oil in a deep non stick pan. Add the crushed green cardamoms, cinnamon, black cardamoms and cloves and sauté till fragrant. Add the boiled onion paste and sauté for five minutes on low heat.

6.  Add khoya and sauté for two to three minutes. Add the kaju-magaz paste and salt and mix well.

7.  Add four cups water, white pepper powder, green chilli paste and green cardamom powder and bring the gravy to a boil. Add ghee and mix well.

8. Strain the gravy into another non stick pan and grind the residue. Add the residue to the strained gravy and mix well. Add mint powder and mix well and bring it to a boil. Add chicken pieces, ginger strips and cream and cook for two to three minutes more.

9. Serve hot, garnished with silver warq and a sprig of mint.

# Chicken Chettinaad

Curry leaves and coconut - two lovely flavours make this dish an absolute winner. Chettinaad cuisine is perhaps the spiciest and most aromatic in the country and has a strong character: freshly ground spices like pepper and chillies mingle with garlic and ginger and liberal amounts of oil to make every preparation a special gift.

## Ingredients

750 grams chicken, cut into 16 pieces on the bone

2 tablespoons oil

15 garlic cloves, chopped

2 medium onions, sliced

⅓ cup tomato puree

¼ cup curry leaves

1½ cups chettinaad masala

Salt to taste

4 tablespoons cashewnut paste

2 tablespoon tamarind pulp

1 teaspoon crushed black peppercorns

4 teaspoons sugar

½ cup chopped fresh coriander leaves

**For chettinaad masala**

¼ cup oil

1 tablespoon cumin seeds

1½ tablespoons black peppercorns

1½ tablespoons coriander seeds

5 green cardamoms

2 one-inch cinnamon sticks

3 cloves

1 star anise

1 tablespoon fennel seeds (saunf)

2 black cardamoms

¼ cup curry leaves

5 dried red chillies

½ cup scraped coconut

10-12 garlic cloves, roughly chopped

2 medium onions, sliced

1 inch ginger piece, roughly chopped

**For garnish**

1 teaspoon scraped coconut

## Method

1.  To make the chettinaad masala, heat the oil in a non stick pan. Add the cumin seeds, black peppercorns, coriander seeds, green cardamoms, cinnamon, cloves, star anise, fennel seeds, black cardamoms, curry leaves, red chillies, coconut, garlic, onions and ginger and sauté for five to seven minutes or till fragrant. Cool and grind to a fine paste with one cup of water. This gives one and half cups of masala.

2.  Heat two tablespoons oil in a deep non stick pan. Add the garlic and onions and sauté for five to seven minutes or till well browned. Add the tomato puree and curry leaves and sauté for a minute. Add the ground masala and sauté for a minute. Add the chicken and sauté for two to three minutes.

3.  Add the salt, cashewnut paste and sauté for a minute. Add the tamarind pulp and one and half cups water and mix well. Cook for three to four minutes.

4.  Add the crushed black peppercorns and sugar and mix well. Cook for three to four minutes or till chicken is completely cooked.

5.  Add the coriander leaves and mix. Serve hot garnished with coconut.

# Kadai Murgh Palak Methi

I remember the kadai was once made from a variety of metals – iron, brass or aluminium. Now, of course, non-stick ware has taken over a lot of the more traditional versions. Palak and methi give extra flavour and nutrition to this variation of kadai chicken. Definitely a must have. Both methi and palak are a favourite in Indian cuisine – they are not just rich in minerals, they are also high in dietary fibre content, and low in calories.

## Ingredients

**For chicken tikka**

400 grams boneless chicken, cut into sixteen 1½ inch pieces

2 teaspoons garlic paste

1 teaspoon ginger paste

2 tablespoons Kashmiri red chilli paste

Salt to taste

½ tablespoon lemon juice

½ cup hung yogurt

1 teaspoon Khazana garam masala powder (see annexure)

1 tablespoon oil

1 teaspoon turmeric powder

1 teaspoon Kashmiri red chilli powder

1 tablespoon gram flour (besan)

Melted butter for basting

**For the gravy**

2 medium onions

2 small bunches (500 grams) fresh spinach leaves, blanched

¼ cup oil

25 garlic cloves, chopped

1⅓ tablespoons kadai masala (see annexure)

Salt to taste

½ cup fresh tomato puree

½ bunch (200 grams) fresh fenugreek leaves, blanched and chopped

½ teaspoon turmeric powder

2 teaspoons Kashmiri red chilli powder

2 teaspoons coriander powder

3 tablespoons butter

1 teaspoon crushed black peppercorns

2 teaspoons chaat masala (see annexure)

2 teaspoons dried fenugreek leaves (kasoori methi)

2 tablespoons cashewnut paste

¼ cup yogurt

1 medium green capsicum, cut into 1-inch pieces

1 medium tomato, cut into 1-inch pieces

¼ cup fresh cream

2 tablespoons chopped fresh coriander leaves

1 teaspoon lemon juice

1 teaspoon red chilli flakes

## Method

1.  To make the chicken tikka, preheat oven to 200°C / 400°F.

2.  Mix together the garlic paste, ginger paste, red chilli paste, salt, lemon juice, hung yogurt and garam masala powder and apply to the chicken pieces.

3.  Heat the oil in a small non stick pan and take it off the heat. Add the turmeric powder, red chilli powder and gram flour and mix well. Add this to the chicken and set aside to marinate for one hour.

4.  Place the chicken pieces on a baking tray and cook in the preheated oven for ten minutes. Baste with melted butter and cook for five minutes more. Set aside.

5.  For the gravy, finely chop one onion and chop the other into one-inch square pieces.

6. Chop two thirds of blanched spinach leaves and make a puree of the remaining spinach leaves.
7. Heat the oil in a non stick kadai, add the garlic and sauté till light brown.
8. Add one tablespoon kadai masala, finely chopped onion and salt and sauté till lightly browned. Add the tomato puree and sauté till oil separates.
9. Add the fenugreek leaves and chopped spinach leaves and sauté for two minutes more.
10. Add the turmeric powder, red chilli powder, coriander powder and butter and sauté for five minutes.
11. Add the crushed black peppercorns, chaat masala, kasoori methi, cashewnut paste, yogurt, spinach puree, onion pieces, capsicum and tomato and mix well.
12. Add the chicken tikkas and cream and cook for two to three minutes.
13. Transfer into a serving dish, sprinkle coriander leaves, remaining kadai masala, lemon juice and red chilli flakes and serve hot.

# Achari Gosht

A great flavour-enriched experience - lamb cooked in special pickling spices. Pickles and preserves are an integral part of any Indian meal and will always be seen on the table. The spice mix is not necessarily hot, but does have a delightful tang that whets the appetite and makes a second helping a must. This dish tastes best when it is served a few hours after it is prepared, simply because the masala becomes more concentrated, and lamb pieces more deeply marinated.

## Ingredients

550 grams boneless mutton, cut into 1 inch pieces

½ cup mustard oil

1½ teaspoons onion seeds (kalonji)

1 teaspoon mustard seeds

1 teaspoon cumin seeds

1 teaspoon fennel seeds (saunf)

4 large onions, chopped

7 green chillies

5 dried red chillies

Salt to taste

2 tablespoons garlic paste

1 tablespoon ginger paste

3 tablespoons achari masala (see annexure)

1 tablespoon turmeric powder

2 tablespoons coriander powder

1 tablespoon crushed black peppercorns

2 cups yogurt, whisked

1 cup tomato puree

½ cup chopped fresh coriander leaves + 1 sprig

½ cup kaju magaz paste (see annexure)

2 tablespoons vinegar

2 teaspoons dried mango powder (amchur)

## Method

1. Heat the mustard oil in a non stick frying pan till it smokes. Let it cool slightly. Heat it again on medium heat and add one teaspoon onion seeds, mustard seeds, cumin seeds and fennel seeds and sauté for two minutes.

2. Add the onions, green chillies and red chillies and sauté for a minute. Add the salt and continue to sauté for eight to ten minutes or till the masala is well browned.

3. Add the mutton, garlic paste and ginger paste and sauté for two minutes. Add two tablespoons achari masala and turmeric powder and sauté, stirring continuously for a minute.

4. Add the coriander powder and sauté, stirring, for ten minutes. Add the crushed peppercorns and mix well.

5. Add the yogurt and mix well. Cook for five minutes, stirring continuously. Add the tomato puree and mix well. Add the coriander leaves and two cups of water and let the gravy come to a boil.

6. Transfer into a pressure cooker and cook under pressure till pressure is released eight times (eight whistles).

7. Open the lid when the pressure reduces completely and transfer the contents of the cooker into a deep non stick pan. Add the kaju magaz paste and vinegar. Mix well. Add the dried mango powder and mix well. Finish off with the remaining achari masala, stir well.

8. Transfer into a serving dish, sprinkle over the remaining onion seeds and serve hot, garnished with a sprig of coriander.

# Mangalorean Fish Curry

Coconuts and curry leaves are the mainstay of Manglorean food. The best part of this cuisine is the intermingling of various spices in the right proportions so that the distinct flavour and taste of each is experienced. Besides this, chillies and coconut with fish makes this dish perfectly authentic Mangalorean.

## Ingredients

450 grams pomfret, cut into darnes

Salt to taste

1 cup scraped coconut

4 medium onions, chopped

4 dried red chillies, roasted

2 teaspoons coriander seeds

1 teaspoon cumin seeds

10-12 black peppercorns

¼ teaspoon fenugreek seeds (methi dana)

½ teaspoon turmeric powder

5 garlic cloves

3 tablespoons oil

12 curry leaves + 1 sprig for garnish

1 teaspoon mustard seeds

1 cup coconut milk

2½ tablespoons tamarind pulp

## Method

1. Pat the fish pieces dry, sprinkle with salt and set aside, preferably in a refrigerator, for one hour.

2. Grind the coconut, half the onions, red chillies, coriander seeds, cumin seeds, peppercorns, fenugreek seeds, turmeric powder and garlic with one cup of water to a smooth paste.

3. Heat the oil in a deep non stick pan, add the curry leaf sprig and fry for a minute or two. Drain and set aside. Add mustard seeds to the oil and when they splutter, add the remaining onions and sauté till golden brown.

4. Add curry leaves and sauté for a minute. Add the ground paste and sauté till oil surfaces.

5. Add coconut milk and cook for three minutes. Add one cup water and tamarind pulp and mix. Cook for two to three minutes.

6. Add salt and the marinated fish and cook for seven to eight minutes.

7. Serve hot, garnished with the fried curry leaf sprig

# Kadai Prawns

Cooking in a kadai is very effective in making a dish quickly while retaining the rich and fresh flavours of the ingredients. Here we have plump prawns cooked in a rich masala - a dish fit for a king.

## Ingredients

4 tablespoons kadai masala (see annexue)

16 medium prawns, peeled and deveined

¼ cup oil

2 medium onions, chopped

2 medium tomatoes, chopped

1 tablespoon ginger paste

2 tablespoons garlic paste

1 teaspoon turmeric powder

2 teaspoons Kashmiri red chilli powder

1 tablespoon coriander powder

2 tablespoons dried fenugreek leaves (kasoori methi)

½ cup tomato puree

Salt to taste

¼ cup kaju-magaz paste (see annexure)

1½ inch ginger piece, chopped

1 medium green capsicum, diced

2 medium tomatoes, diced

1 large onion, diced and layers separated

1 tablespoon chopped fresh coriander leaves

## Method

1. Heat the oil in a non stick kadai. Add two tablespoons kadai masala and sauté for one minute.

2. Add the onions and cook till lightly browned. Add the tomatoes and cook till they soften.

3. Add the ginger and garlic pastes and sauté for a minute. Add the turmeric powder, red chilli powder, coriander powder and one tablespoon kasoori methi and sauté for two to three minutes.

4. Add the tomato puree and mix well and cook till the oil surfaces.

5. Add the salt, kaju-magaz paste and sauté for five minutes. Add ginger and sauté for two minutes.

6. Add the remaining kadai masala, capsicum, tomatoes, onion and prawns and cook on high heat, stirring, for five minutes.

7. Add the remaining kasoori methi and mix. Serve hot garnished with coriander leaves.

## Chef's note

For Kadai Masala, coarsely grind together 4 tablespoons coriander seeds, 20-25 black peppercorns, 7 green cardamoms, 2 dried red chillies, 1 black cardamom and 1 tablespoon cumin seeds. This makes 7 tablespoons of powder.

# Keema Hari Mirch do Pyaaza

'Do' means 'two' and 'pyaaza' refers to 'onions'... and so 'do pyaaza' means a dish with onions added in two ways. Some onions are cooked the regular way with ginger and garlic and rest of the masalas, while some are more visible and retain their crunch. While buying the green chillies, one should look out for those are crisp and bright, with no wrinkles, spots or soft patches.

## Ingredients

500 grams minced mutton (keema)

14 green chillies (light green variety)

6 medium onions, chopped

¼ cup + 4 tablespoons oil

1 tablespoon crushed black peppercorns

3 teaspoons Khazana garam masala powder (see annexure)

Salt to taste

5 teaspoons coriander powder

4 teaspoons red chilli powder

1 teaspoon green cardamom powder

1½ inch ginger piece, chopped

25-30 garlic cloves, chopped

2 medium tomatoes, chopped

1 teaspoon turmeric powder

¼ cup + 4 teaspoons chopped fresh coriander leaves

1 large onion, quartered and layers separated

2 tablespoons chopped fresh mint leaves

## Method

1. Slit ten green chillies and finely chop the remaining four.

2. Heat one fourth cup oil in a non stick kadai, add the slit green chillies, two cups chopped onions and sauté for three minutes. Add crushed black peppercorns and sauté till the onions are well browned.

3. Add garam masala powder, keema and salt and sauté for five minutes.

4. Add three teaspoons coriander powder and three teaspoons red chilli powder and sauté for ten to fifteen minutes. Add the green cardamom powder and mix well.

5. Heat four tablespoons oil in another non stick pan, add the ginger, garlic and chopped green chillies and sauté for two minutes. Add the remaining chopped onions and sauté till they are well browned. Add the tomatoes and salt and sauté till they soften.

6. Add the turmeric powder and the remaining red chilli powder and sauté for a minute. Add the remaining coriander powder and sauté for five minutes. Add quarter cup of water and two teaspoons chopped coriander leaves and mix.

7. Add the quartered onion and sauté for five minutes. Add the cooked keema and mix well. Add one and a quarter cups of water and adjust salt and cook till all the water is absorbed and the keema is completely cooked.

8. Add a quarter cup coriander leaves and mint leaves and mix well.

9. Transfer the keema into a serving dish, garnish with the remaining coriander leaves and serve hot.

# Laziz Murgh Tikka Masala

In Urdu laziz means luscious. This is one recipe that best epitomises my restaurant food. It is rather elaborate, but once you get to cooking it you will willy nilly follow the steps simply because you will be so eager to taste the result. The dish is worth all the appreciation it will get - tasty, spicy, succulent. Best had with naan.

## Ingredients

**For murgh tikka**

400 grams boneless chicken, cut into 16 pieces

3 teaspoons garlic paste

1½ teaspoons ginger paste

3½ teaspoons lemon juice

2 tablespoons Kashmiri red chilli paste

1 teaspoon + ¾ tablespoon Kashmiri red chilli powder

Salt to taste

1½ tablespoons oil

¼ teaspoon carom seeds (ajwain)

½ tablespoon gram flour (besan)

½ teaspoon turmeric powder

½ teaspoon Khazana garam masala powder (see annexure)

½ cup yogurt

1 teaspoon red chilli flakes

½ teaspoon black salt

Butter for basting

**For gravy**

¼ cup oil

25 garlic cloves, chopped

1½ inch ginger piece, chopped

2 medium onions, chopped

Salt to taste

2 medium tomatoes, chopped

1 cup tomato puree

1 tablespoon coriander powder

1 teaspoon turmeric powder

1 teaspoon green cardamom powder

1 teaspoon Khazana garam masala powder (see annexure)

¼ cup cashewnut paste

1 tablespoon Kashmiri red chilli powder

1 tablespoon kadai masala (see annexure)

1 large green capsicum, cut into 1 inch pieces

1 large onion, cut into 1 inch pieces

1 large tomato, cut into 1 inch pieces

3 tablespoons butter

1 tablespoon dried fenugreek leaves (kasoori methi)

¼ cup grated khoya/mawa

½ cup + 2 teaspoons fresh cream

2 teaspoons honey

## Method

1. Mix two teaspoons garlic paste, one teaspoon ginger paste, two teaspoons lemon juice, two tablespoons red chilli paste, one teaspoon red chilli powder and salt in a bowl. Add the chicken pieces and mix well. Set aside to marinate for thirty minutes.

2. Heat the oil in a small non stick pan. Add the carom seeds and remove the pan from the heat. Add the gram flour and mix well. Add the turmeric powder, three fourth tablespoon red chilli powder and garam masala powder and mix. Add this to yogurt and mix till smooth.

3. Add red chilli flakes, one teaspoon garlic paste, half teaspoon ginger paste, salt, black salt and one and half teaspoons lemon juice and mix well.

4. Add the marinated chicken pieces and mix well. Set aside to marinate for thirty minutes more.

5. Preheat the oven to 250ºC / 475ºF.

6. String the chicken pieces onto skewers and cook in the preheated oven for ten minutes.

7. Remove from the oven, baste with butter and cook for two to three minutes more. Remove and set aside to cool.

8. For the gravy, heat the oil in a deep non stick pan. Add the

garlic, ginger and sauté for two to three minutes. Add the onions and sauté till brown. Add the salt and mix.

9. Add the tomatoes and sauté for five minutes. Add the tomato puree and mix and sauté for four to five minutes.

10. Add the coriander powder, turmeric powder, cardamom powder and garam masala powder and sauté for two to three minutes.

11. Add the cashewnut paste, red chilli powder, kadai masala, green capsicum, onion, tomato and one cup water and mix well. Cook for two to three minutes.

12. Add the butter and kasoori methi powder and mix. Add the chicken tikka, khoya and one cup water and cook till the gravy comes to a boil.

13. Add half cup of fresh cream and mix. Add the honey and mix well and cook for five to seven minutes.

14. Serve hot garnished with a swirl of cream.

# Murgh Makhni

Makhni can mean two things when it comes to food: it could be as smooth as butter or it could mean cooked in lots of butter. Here it is both – quite a bit of butter is used to get the smooth and velvety gravy. The sourness of the tomatoes gets cleverly masked by the honey and the dried fenugreek leaves bring out the Moghlai flavours. Murgh Makhni is one of the top selling dishes in Indian restaurants not only in India but outside it too. We do get incredulous guests asking 'what do you do to your makhni gravy? It is so smooth and tasty!" Well, now you know.

## Ingredients

**For murgh tikka**

400 grams boneless chicken, cut into 16 pieces

3 teaspoons garlic paste

1½ teaspoons ginger paste

3½ teaspoons lemon juice

2 tablespoons Kashmiri red chilli paste

1 teaspoon + ¾ tablespoon Kashmiri red chilli powder

Salt to taste

1½ tablespoons oil

¼ teaspoon carom seeds (ajwain)

½ tablespoon gram flour (besan)

½ teaspoon turmeric powder

¾ tablespoon Kashmiri red chilli powder

½ teaspoon Khazana garam masala powder (see annexure)

½ cup yogurt

1 teaspoon red chilli flakes

½ teaspoon black salt

Butter for basting

**For makhni gravy**

500 grams tomatoes, quartered

7-8 garlic cloves

1½ inch ginger piece, roughly chopped

7 green cardamoms

½ blade mace

2 tablespoons red chilli (deghi mirch) powder

100 grams butter

Salt to taste

1½ teaspoons dried fenugreek leaves (kasoori methi) powder

1 tablespoon honey

¼ cup fresh cream

1 teaspoon Khazana garam masala powder (see annexure)

**For garnish**

2 teaspoons fresh cream

1 sprig fresh coriander leaves

## Method

1. Mix two teaspoons garlic paste, one teaspoon ginger paste, two teaspoons lemon juice, red chilli paste, one teaspoon red chilli powder and salt in a bowl. Add the chicken pieces and mix well. Set aside to marinate for thirty minutes, preferably in a refrigerator.

2. Heat the oil in a small non stick pan. Add the carom seeds and remove the pan from the heat. Add the gram flour and mix well. Add the turmeric powder, three-fourth tablespoon red chilli powder and garam masala powder and mix. Add this to the yogurt and mix till smooth.

3. Add the red chilli flakes, one teaspoon garlic paste, half teaspoon ginger paste, salt, black salt and one and a half teaspoons lemon juice and mix well.

4. Add the marinated chicken pieces and mix well. Set aside in the refrigerator to marinate for thirty minutes more.

5. Preheat oven to 250ºC / 475ºF.

6. String the chicken pieces onto skewers and cook in the preheated oven for ten minutes.

7. Remove from the oven, baste with butter and cook for two to three minutes more. Remove and set aside to cool.

8. Heat a deep non stick pan. Add the tomatoes, garlic, ginger, green cardamoms, mace, one cup water, red chilli powder and butter and let it boil for fifteen minutes.

9. Add the salt and mix well. Take the pan off the heat and allow it to cool.

10. Blend the gravy to a fine puree, strain into another deep non stick pan and cook for five minutes.

11. Add the tikkas and kasoori methi powder and honey and cook for two to three minutes more. Add the cream and garam masala powder and mix lightly.

12. Transfer into a serving dish, garnish with a swirl of fresh cream and a coriander sprig and serve hot.

# Puran Singh da Tariwala Murgh

The Puran Singh da Dhaba on the Ambala-Delhi GT road is almost a pilgrimage spot for foodies, since nine times out of ten people stop there to savour the delicious chicken curry. This is our version - we have tried to capture that magic, but with our spell. We have often been told that our curry is better than the original! But we are modest and give full credit to the dhaba favourite.

## Ingredients

750 grams chicken, cut into 16 pieces on the bone

¼ cup oil

2 one-inch cinnamon sticks

5 green cardamoms

1 teaspoon cumin seeds

2 black cardamoms

4 medium onions, sliced

Salt to taste

1 tablespoon ginger paste

2 tablespoon garlic paste

1 cup browned onions

1 teaspoon turmeric powder

2 teaspoons Kashmiri red chilli powder

5 teaspoons coriander powder

4 teaspoons Khazana garam masala powder (see annexure)

1 cup fresh tomato puree

1 teaspoon green cardamom powder

8 green chillies, chopped

½ cup + 1 tablespoon chopped fresh coriander leaves

1½ inch ginger pieces, chopped

1 teaspoon red chilli (deghi mirch) powder

## Method

1. Heat the oil in a deep non stick pan, add the cinnamon, green cardamoms, cumin seeds and black cardamoms and sauté for two minutes. Add the onions and sauté till lightly browned.

2. Add the salt, ginger paste and garlic paste and sauté for two to three minutes

3. Add the browned onions, turmeric powder, red chilli powder, four teaspoons coriander powder and three teaspoons garam masala powder and sauté for two minutes.

4. Add the tomato puree and chicken and sauté for four to five minutes.

5. Add the green cardamom powder and sauté for two to three minutes more. Add the green chillies and half cup coriander leaves and sauté for five minutes.

6. Add two cups water and mix well. Cook for ten minutes on medium heat.

7. Add the ginger, remaining coriander powder, red chilli powder and remaining garam masala powder and mix well.

8. Take the pan off the heat, remove the chicken pieces and strain the gravy into another deep non stick pan and add the chicken pieces.

9. Grind the residue and add to the gravy and bring it to a boil. Let it simmer for four to five minutes.

10. Serve hot, garnished with coriander leaves

# Raan Buzkazi

While the preparation is elaborate and cooking itself takes a very long time, the end result is worth all the effort. And the presentation is spectacular, a feast for the eyes as well as the stomach! Whole leg of lamb marinated in spicy masala, slow baked till tender and served in spicy gravy. This dish has been made popular by restaurants. Choose a leg from a young lamb because the meat is tender and will cook faster.

## Ingredients

1 kilogram leg of goat or lamb

1 medium onion, sliced

8-10 garlic cloves

8-10 green cardamoms

2-3 one-inch cinnamon sticks

For marinade

2 tablespoons raw papaya paste (papaya ground with skin)

2 tablespoons garlic paste

1 tablespoon ginger paste

1 tablespoon red chilli powder

2 tablespoons red chilli paste

Salt to taste

For gravy

¼ cup butter

½ cup chicken stock

¼ cup browned onions

½ cup yogurt

1 teaspoon roasted chana powder

1 teaspoon Khazana garam masala powder (see annexure)

2 inch ginger piece, cut into thin strips

¼ cup chopped fresh mint leaves

¼ cup chopped fresh coriander leaves

For garnish

1 large onion, cut into rings

2 tablespoons chopped fresh coriander leaves

## Method

1. Clean the leg of lamb and make small slashes in the meat with a knife. Combine the papaya paste, garlic paste, ginger paste, red chilli powder, red chilli paste and salt and apply it on the leg. Place the leg on a deep baking tray and keep it in a refrigerator to marinate for three to four hours.

2. Preheat oven to 250ºC/ 475ºF.

3. Put the onion, garlic, green cardamoms, cinnamon and four cups of water over the leg of lamb and cover it with aluminium foil. Keep the tray in the preheated oven and bake for four to five hours.

4. Remove the tray from the oven. Take the lamb leg out of the tray and separate the meat from the bone and cut into big pieces. Retain the bone. Strain the stock into a bowl.

5. For the gravy heat the butter in a non stick pan, add the strained stock and chicken stock and cook till it is reduced to half its original quantity.

6. Add the browned onions, yogurt, roasted chana powder and garam masala powder and mix well. Cook for five minutes and strain the sauce into another non stick pan.

7. Add the ginger, mint leaves and coriander leaves and cook for ten to fifteen minutes on medium heat.

8. Add the mutton pieces and mix well.

9. Place the bone on a platter in an upright position and pour the gravy along with the mutton around it.

10. Garnish with onion rings and coriander leaves and serve hot.

# Nalli Rogan Josh

This dish was originally brought to Kashmir by the Moghals. 'Rogan' means 'oil' or 'red' in Persian, and 'josh' means 'heat' or 'passion'. And while the colour of this dish is a fiery red, it is only mildly hot, made with Kashmiri chillies which are more about colour than heat. This dish is a hot seller in our restaurants. Fennel and ginger dominate and give the curry a touch of the exotic. The final look of this curry is eye catching – ruby red gravy with a thin film of oil on top.

## Ingredients

500 grams mutton shanks (nalli)
200 grams boneless mutton, cut into 1 inch pieces
½ cup oil
10 green cardamoms
2 one-inch cinnamon sticks
1½ tablespoons fennel seeds (saunf)
5 cloves
6 medium onions, sliced
Salt to taste
2 tablespoons ginger-garlic paste
4 teaspoons fennel powder
4 teaspoons green cardamom powder
2 tablespoons Kashmiri red chilli powder
1 cup yogurt, whisked
1 tablespoon roasted chana powder
1 tablespoon chopped fresh coriander leaves
2 inch ginger piece, cut into thin strips
For garnishing
2 tablespoons chopped fresh coriander leaves
1 inch ginger piece, cut into thin strips

## Method

1. Heat the oil in a deep non stick pan, add the green cardamoms, cinnamon, fennel seeds and cloves and sauté for half a minute.

2. Add the onions, salt and sauté till well browned. Add the ginger-garlic paste and sauté for a minute.

3. Add the mutton shanks and boneless mutton pieces and sauté till lightly browned. Add three teaspoons fennel powder, three teaspoons green cardamom powder, Kashmiri red chilli powder and yogurt and sauté till the oil separates.

4. Add two cups of water and mix well. Transfer into a pressure cooker and cook under pressure till pressure is released five times (five whistles) or for around twenty minutes.

5. Open the lid when the pressure reduces completely. Remove the mutton pieces and strain the gravy into a deep non stick pan.

6. Boil the gravy, add the mutton pieces and mix. Mix roasted chana powder with four tablespoons of water and add to the gravy and mix well. Add the remaining green cardamom powder, coriander leaves and ginger strips and simmer for five minutes. Add the remaining fennel powder and mix well.

7. Transfer into a serving bowl, garnish with coriander leaves and ginger strips and serve hot.

## Note

Ideally this dish should be slow cooked in a pan - cover the pan with a lid and seal with whole wheat flour dough and cook on dum till done. But this takes a long time. Since the masala has to be stirred and sautéed and it is difficult to do so in a pressure cooker, we have first sautéed the masala in a pan and then transferred it into a pressure cooker to cook the mutton faster.

# Mutton Pepper Fry

A touch of Southern spice – black peppercorns and loads of curry leaves. Just go for it, especially if you like all things hot and happening. Pepper is perhaps one of the oldest spices used in Indian cuisine. The Malabar coast in Kerala is the main growing region for what is still called 'black gold', once a popular trading commodity.

## Ingredients

550 grams boneless mutton, cut into 1 inch cubes
¼ cup oil
1 sprig of curry leaves
2 medium onions, sliced
6 dried red chillies
1 tablespoon ginger paste
2 tablespoons garlic paste
Salt to taste
1 tablespoon crushed black peppercorns
1 teaspoon turmeric powder
1 teaspoon red chilli (deghi mirch) powder
1½ tablespoons coriander powder
¼ cup chopped fresh coriander leaves
½ teaspoon sugar
1 tablespoon tamarind pulp
For paste
½ tablespoon oil
½ teaspoon caraway seeds (shahi jeera)
15 black peppercorns
1 star anise
3 green cardamoms
1 black cardamom
½ inch cinnamon stick
2 cloves
1 tablespoon coriander seeds
10-12 curry leaves
3-4 garlic cloves, chopped
½ inch ginger, chopped
½ medium onion, sliced

1 cup + 2 tablespoons scraped coconut
1 teaspoon red chilli (deghi mirch) powder
½ teaspoon turmeric powder
1 teaspoon coriander powder

## Method

1. Heat the oil in a pressure cooker, add the curry leaf sprig and fry till crisp. Drain and set aside for garnishing. Add the onions and sauté on medium heat for five minutes or till translucent. Add the red chillies, ginger paste and garlic paste and sauté for a minute. Add the mutton pieces, salt and crushed peppercorns and sauté for eight to ten minutes.

2. Add the turmeric powder, red chilli powder and coriander powder and sauté for a minute. Add two cups of water and mix. Close the cooker with the lid and cook on low heat for twenty five to thirty minutes or till the pressure is released three times (three whistles).

3. For the paste, heat half tablespoon oil in a non stick pan. Add the caraway seeds, black peppercorns, star anise, green cardamoms, black cardamom, cinnamon, cloves, coriander seeds, curry leaves, garlic, ginger and onion and sauté for a minute. Add half cup coconut and sauté for two minutes. Add red chilli powder, turmeric powder and coriander powder and sauté for three minutes. Take the pan off the heat and set aside to cool. Grind with five tablespoons water to a smooth paste.

4. Heat a deep non stick pan, add the ground paste and the cooked mutton and mix well. Once it comes to a boil, add the coriander leaves and mix. Continue to cook, stirring, for four to five minutes or till it becomes semi dry.

5. Add half cup coconut and mix well and cook for two minutes or till thick. Add the sugar and tamarind pulp and mix.

6. Serve hot, garnished with the remaining coconut and the fried sprig of curry leaves.

Chef's tip: Adding little salt while sautéing onions will help to soften them faster without burning.

# Rice & Rotis

# Rice & Rotis

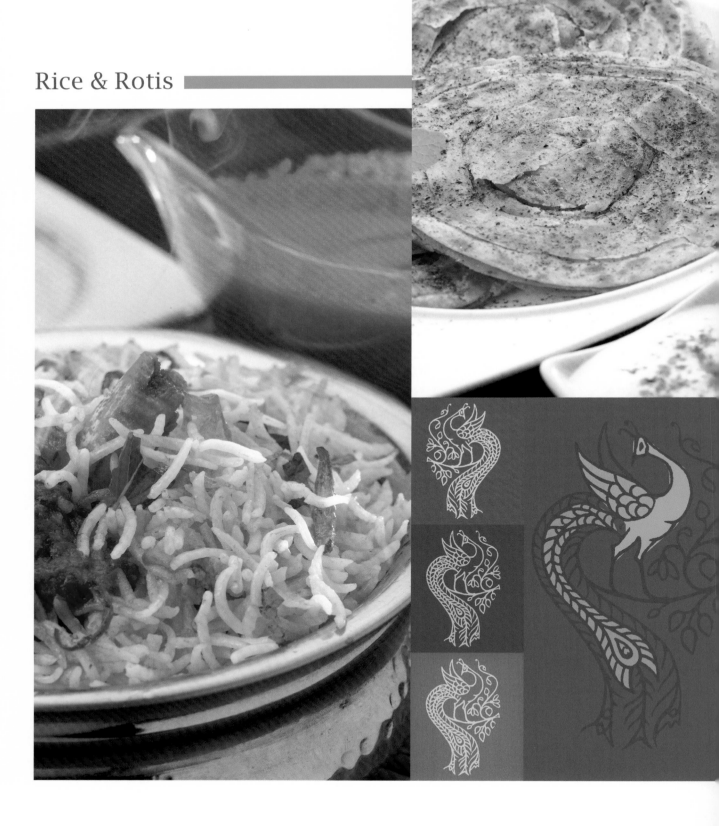

# Lachcha Parantha

Paranthas, rotis, puris – the unleavened breads of India have become popular all over the world today. They are perfect for eating with the highly spiced and flavourful curries and stews of the north, where they originate from, and can be made in various forms. The lachcha parantha, also known as multi-layered Indian bread, is flaky and deliciously fragile. It is a bit tricky to make, but very tasty, with several crisp layers.

## Ingredients

2½ cups whole wheat flour (atta) + for dusting

½ cup refined flour (maida)

Salt to taste

8 teaspoons pure ghee + for shallow frying

## Method

1. Combine both the flours with salt and one and a half cups of water in a bowl and knead into a soft dough. Cover with a damp cloth and rest for about fifteen minutes.

2. Divide into eight equal portions. Roll out each portion into a thin chapatti. Spread one teaspoon ghee on it and dust with a little flour. Make small pleats and then roll into a roundel. Let them rest for ten minutes.

3. Roll out each roundel into a slightly thick parantha of five to six inch diameter.

4. Heat a non stick tawa and place a parantha on it. Drizzle with a little ghee, turn it over and drizzle some more ghee and cook till both the sides are golden brown.

5. Crush lightly with your hands to open out the layers and serve hot.

# Aloo Anardana Kulcha

Anardana or pomegranate seeds are the star attraction here. They give their tartness only when crushed or ground and are rarely used whole. This kulcha goes very well with chholay. At banquets it is cooked live as the guests watch. With imli ki chutney, onion lachcha and green chillies, it's simply irresistible.

## Ingredients

3 cups refined flour (maida)

1 teaspoon baking powder

1 teaspoon sugar

Salt to taste

5 tablespoons butter + for basting

1 cup milk

### For stuffing

3 large potatoes, boiled, peeled and mashed

1 teaspoon crushed dried pomegranate seeds (anardana)

1 teaspoon Khazana garam masala powder (see annexure)

4 green chillies, chopped

2 tablespoons chopped fresh coriander leaves

1½ teaspoons chaat masala (see annexure)

1½ teaspoons red chilli powder

1 medium onion, chopped

## Method

1.  Mix together the refined flour and baking powder in a bowl.

2.  Mix sugar, salt, butter and milk and add to the flour and knead into a soft dough. Cover with a damp cloth and set aside for forty minutes.

3.  Preheat oven to 200°C / 400°F.

4.  For the stuffing mix together potatoes, garam masala powder, green chillies, coriander leaves, chaat masala, red chilli powder, pomegranate seeds and onion.

5.  Divide both the dough and the stuffing into eight equal portions. Roll each dough portion into a ball, spread it slightly on your palm and place a portion of the stuffing on it; close in the edges and press lightly to seal.

6.  Roll the balls out into thick rotis of five to six inches in diameter. Place the rotis, two at a time, on a baking tray and bake, basting with butter, for eight minutes.

7.  Serve hot.

# Hyderabadi Dum Gosht Biryani

Dum cooking was revived in India in 1783 by Nawab Asaf-ud-Daulah during the construction of the Bara Imam Bara mosque in Delhi. The food for construction workers was par-cooked in large clay pots; the mouth of each pot was covered with a clay saucer and sealed with a paste of flour to prevent the steam from escaping. Many people find it difficult to believe that uncooked mutton can be finished with half cooked rice. Yes, it is not only possible, but the end result will leave you completely amazed. It definitely is the greatest ever treat from the royal kitchens of Hyderabad.

## Ingredients

500 grams mutton, cut into 1 inch pieces on the bone

2½ cups Basmati rice, washed and soaked for ½ hour

½ tablespoon ginger paste

1 tablespoon garlic paste

3 tablespoons raw papaya paste (papaya ground with skin)

Salt to taste

½ tablespoon turmeric powder

1½ tablespoons red chilli powder

1½ tablespoons biryani masala (see annexure)

¼ cup melted pure ghee

¼ cup + 2 tablespoons fresh mint leaves, torn

4-5 green chillies, slit

1 inch ginger piece, cut into thin strips

½ cup yogurt, whisked

A few saffron strands

½ tablespoon warm milk

3 green cardamoms

3 cloves

1 black cardamom

1 inch cinnamon stick

2 tablespoons melted butter

2 tablespoons fresh cream

2 tablespoons browned onions

Whole wheat dough (atta) to seal

## Method

1.  In a bowl mix together the mutton, ginger paste, garlic paste, papaya paste, salt, turmeric powder, half tablespoon red chilli powder and half tablespoon biryani masala. Cover the bowl with cling film and set it in a refrigerator to marinate for four hours.

2.  Take the bowl out of the refrigerator and add melted ghee and mix well. Add one tablespoon biryani masala, one tablespoon red chilli powder, quarter cup mint leaves, salt, green chillies, ginger strips and yogurt and mix well. Set aside in the refrigerator to marinate for another hour.

3.  Dissolve the saffron in warm milk in a small bowl and set aside.

4.  Boil seven cups of water in a deep non stick pan. Add the green cardamoms, cloves, black cardamom, cinnamon and salt and let it boil for a few minutes. Remove the whole spices. Drain the soaked rice and add and cook for five minutes. Drain well.

5.  Arrange the marinated mutton in another deep non stick pan and top it with the rice.

6.  Mix melted butter with cream and pour this over the rice. Drizzle the saffron milk and sprinkle browned onions and remaining mint leaves.

7.  Cover the pan with a lid and seal the edges with whole wheat dough.

8.  Cook over low heat for half an hour. Let it stand for five to ten minutes. Break open the seal and serve the biryani hot with a raita of your choice.

# Peshawari Naan

Naan is a form of leavened bread that has become popular all over the world. It is the perfect accompaniment to the highly flavoured curries of North Indian cuisine, and can be adapted to become a delightful wrapping for kebabs, dry stir-fries and all sorts of fillings. Naan can be flavoured with almost anything, sweet or savoury, and cooks in seconds in a tandoor. This is a rich, exotic and sweeter variation of the naan and can be prepared either stuffed with nuts or coated with them. What we have here is naan with a generous coating of pistachios, sesame seeds and melon seeds that makes it distinct from other versions of this bread.

## Ingredients

3 cups refined flour (maida)

1 teaspoon yeast

3 teaspoons castor sugar

1 teaspoon baking powder

1 teaspoon salt

1 cup + 1 tablespoon milk

2 tablespoons butter + for brushing

¼ cup coarsely ground pistachios

¼ cup white sesame seeds (safed til)

¼ cup onion seeds (kalonji)

¼ cup melon seeds (magaz)

## Method

1. Mix together the yeast and one teaspoon castor sugar in one tablespoon water and stir till they blend well.

2. Sieve the refined flour, baking powder, remaining castor sugar and salt into a bowl. Add the yeast mixture and mix. Add milk and 2 tablespoons butter and knead into a soft dough. Cover with a damp cloth and rest for fifteen to twenty minutes.

3. Meanwhile preheat oven to 250°C / 475°F.

4. Mix together pistachios, white sesame seeds, onion seeds and melon seeds.

5. Divide the dough into eight equal portions and shape into balls. Pat each of them into roundels with your finger tips and pull one side to give it a triangular shape.

6. Coat one side of the naans with the pistachio mixture. Place them on a greased baking tray and bake in the preheated oven for ten to twelve minutes or till light brown.

7. Brush with butter and serve hot.

# Nizami Tarkari Biryani

Much of our Indian cuisine is vegetarian, using the freshness of vegetables rather than the heavy intensity of meats. This recipe from the Nizam's kitchen has a medley of fresh vegetables cooked with flavourful Basmati rice. Don't get overwhelmed with the array of spices - after all, it is something that is fit for royalty. It is delicious with raita and a few crunchies like papads or chips and makes for perfect comfort food.

## Ingredients

2 medium carrots, cut into diamonds and blanched

12-14 French beans, cut into diamonds and blanched

1 cup shelled green peas, blanched

150 grams cauliflower, separated into small florets, blanched

10 baby corns, cut into diamonds

2½ cups Basmati rice, soaked

Salt to taste

3 green cardamoms

2 one-inch cinnamon sticks

4 bay leaves

¼ cup oil

1 tablespoon caraway seeds (shahi jeera)

1 medium onion, chopped

1 tablespoon garlic paste

½ tablespoon ginger paste

5 crushed green cardamoms

4 crushed cloves

½ cup tomato puree

1 teaspoon turmeric powder

2 teaspoons coriander powder

3 teaspoons green cardamom powder

2 teaspoons red chilli powder

½ cup yogurt

3 one-inch ginger pieces, cut into thin strips

5 green chillies, cut into thin strips

¾ cup + 2 tablespoons browned onions

½ cup fresh mint leaves

⅓ cup + ¼ cup chopped fresh coriander leaves + to garnish

2 tablespoons screw pine (kewda) water

A generous pinch of saffron

1¾ tablespoons butter

4 teaspoons cream

Whole wheat dough (atta) to seal

## Method

1. Drain and cook the rice in five cups of water with salt, three green cardamoms, one inch cinnamon stick and two bay leaves till three fourths done. Drain, discard the whole spices and spread the rice out on a plate to cool.

2. Heat the oil in a deep non stick pan, add the caraway seeds and sauté till they change colour.

3. Add the onions, garlic paste, ginger paste, crushed cardamoms, one inch cinnamon stick, crushed cloves and two bay leaves and sauté for five minutes.

4. Add the tomato puree and quarter cup water and sauté till oil surfaces. Add the turmeric powder, coriander powder, two teaspoons green cardamom powder, red chilli powder, salt and yogurt and sauté for five minutes longer.

5. Add most of the ginger strips and green chilli strips and sauté for five minutes.

6. Add the carrot, French beans, green peas, cauliflower, baby corns and sauté for ten minutes.

7. Add one cup water and half cup browned onions and cook for ten minutes.

8. Add one teaspoon green cardamom powder, quarter cup mint leaves, one third cup coriander leaves and half cup water and cook for five minutes.

9. Add the kewda water and mix. Spread the cooked rice over the vegetables. Sprinkle over one-fourth cup browned onions, remaining mint leaves, remaining ginger strips and quarter cup coriander leaves.

10. Mix saffron with butter and cream, add quarter cup water and mix well. Sprinkle this mixture over the rice.

11. Cover the pan with a lid and seal it with the dough. Cook on dum on low heat for ten to fifteen minutes.

12. Serve hot garnished with coriander leaves and the remaining browned onions.

# Pudina Parantha

The quintessential paranthas with the flavour of mint. Mint is a refreshing addition to almost anything and does well with the blandness of bread. In this recipe, dried mint – which has an intensity of flavor that is stronger than its fresh original – spikes the gentle taste of the parantha, while the fresh leaves chopped into the dough add a special cooling touch. This parantha with Lalla Mussa Dal is our favourite combination, of course!

## Ingredients

2½ cups whole-wheat flour (atta) + for dusting

½ cup refined flour (maida)

4 tablespoons dried mint leaves

Salt to taste

½ cup chopped fresh mint leaves

8 tablespoons ghee

1 tablespoon chaat masala (see annexure)

## Method

1. Combine whole wheat flour, refined flour, two tablespoons dried mint leaves and salt in a large bowl. Add fresh mint leaves and one cup water and knead into a soft dough. Cover with a damp cloth and rest for half an hour.

2. Divide the dough into eight equal portions, cover with a damp cloth and rest for ten minutes.

3. Roll out each dough portion into a roundel of eight inch diameter, apply one teaspoon ghee all over, sprinkle a little dry flour, make small pleats and then roll into a roundel. Let them rest for ten minutes.

4. Grind together the remaining dried mint leaves and chaat masala.

5. Heat a non stick tawa.

6. Roll out the dough roundels into eight inch round paranthas. Cook them on the hot tawa, one at a time, applying one teaspoon ghee on either side till both the sides are cooked and crisp.

7. Sprinkle the mint leaves-chaat masala powder over each parantha and serve hot.

# Mumbai Mast Tomato Pulao

A taste of Mumbai's street food - sadak chhaap tomato tawa pulao redolent with pav bhaji masala.

## Ingredients

8 medium tomatoes

3 cups cooked rice

3½ tablespoons oil

1 tablespoon cumin seeds

1 medium onion, chopped

½ tablespoon ginger paste

1 tablespoon garlic paste

⅓ cup shelled green peas, boiled and crushed

1 medium green capsicum, finely chopped

2 tablespoons Khazana Pav Bhaji Masala (see annexure)

4 teaspoons red chilli paste

Salt to taste

7 tablespoons chopped fresh coriander leaves

2 tablespoons lemon juice

## Method

1. Dice three tomatoes and puree the remaining five.

2. Heat the oil in a non stick pan and add cumin seeds. When they begin to change colour add the onion and sauté till lightly browned. Add the ginger paste, garlic paste and tomato puree and sauté till the mixture thickens. Add the diced tomatoes and cook till the tomatoes soften.

3. Add green peas, capsicum, Khazana Pav Bhaji Masala and red chilli paste and mix well. Cook for two to three minutes. Add half cup of water and cook.

4. Add the rice and salt and mix. Add half of the coriander leaves and lemon juice and mix well. Cook on high heat for a couple of minutes.

5. Serve hot garnished with the remaining coriander leaves.

# Chef's tip

You can add half tablespoon vinegar while boiling the rice. This makes the rice whiter and also strengthens the grains when cooked.

# Murgh Noormahal Biryani

A salute to royal cuisine. Chicken pieces cooked in yogurt and a special blend of spices, layered with parboiled basmati rice and finished on low heat is what makes this biryani an out-and-out winner. Each rice grain should be separate, yet bound to its kin by flavour. Overall, this is a pot full of flavours, with a marvellous texture.

## Ingredients

750 grams chicken, cut into 16 pieces on the bone

¼ cup ghee

1 tablespoon caraway seeds (shahi jeera)

4 cloves

7 crushed green cardamoms

1 inch crushed cinnamon stick

2 medium onions, sliced

5 green chillies, slit

1 tablespoon ginger paste

2 tablespoons garlic paste

Salt to taste

2½ tablespoons biryani masala (see annexure)

¼ teaspoon turmeric powder

1 teaspoon coriander powder

2 teaspoons Kashmiri red chilli powder

1¼ cups browned onions

¾ cup yogurt

1 cup fresh mint leaves

1 tablespoon lemon juice

½ cup chopped fresh coriander leaves

2 tablespoons screw pine (kewda) water

3 tablespoons rose water

2 tablespoons butter

2 tablespoons cream

A generous pinch of saffron

2 inch ginger piece, cut into thin strips

1 sprig fresh mint leaves

Whole wheat dough (atta) to seal

### For the rice

2½ cups Basmati rice, soaked

4 green cardamoms

2 black cardamoms

1 bay leaf

4 cloves

½ tablespoon rose water

2 teaspoons lemon juice

## Method

1. Heat the ghee in a deep non stick pan, add the caraway seeds, cloves, green cardamoms and cinnamon and sauté till fragrant. Add the onions and sauté for five to seven minutes or till well browned.

2. Add the green chillies, ginger paste and garlic paste and sauté for two minutes. Add the chicken, salt and biryani masala and cook for five minutes.

3. Add the turmeric powder, coriander powder and red chilli powder and cook for two to three minutes.

4. Add half cup browned onions and mix well. Add the yogurt, half cup mint leaves, lemon juice, coriander leaves, kewda water and two tablespoons rose water and mix well.

5. Meanwhile, to cook the rice, boil five cups of water with green cardamoms, black cardamoms, bay leaf and cloves in a deep non stick pan. Drain and add the rice and let it cook till half done. Add the rose water and lemon juice and mix. Strain the rice and reserve the water.

6. Spread the rice over the chicken evenly.

7. Dissolve saffron in two tablespoons lukewarm water and add butter, cream and three fourth cup of the

reserved rice water and mix well. Drizzle this mixture all over the rice.

8. Sprinkle half cup mint leaves, half cup browned onions and ginger strips and cover the pan with a well fitting lid. Seal the edges with dough. Place the pan on a heated tawa and cook on medium heat for twenty minutes.

9. Let it stand for five minutes. Open the lid and sprinkle on the remaining rose water and browned onions. Garnish with mint sprig and serve hot.

# Nimbu Jeera Pulao

Perfect accompaniment for every dal – fluffy basmati rice with lemony twist and cumin.

## Ingredients

1½ cups Basmati rice, soaked
5½ tablespoons ghee
1 bay leaf
1 inch cinnamon stick
2 green cardamoms
1 mace blade
1 star anise
4 cloves
Salt to taste
3 teaspoons cumin seeds
½ teaspoon mustard seeds
1 teaspoon split Bengal gram (chana dal)
15 curry leaves
¼ teaspoon turmeric powder
4 teaspoons lemon juice
1 sprig fresh coriander leaves

## Method

1. Heat one and half tablespoons ghee in a deep non stick pan, add the bay leaf, cinnamon, green cardamoms, mace, star anise and cloves and sauté for half a minute.

2. Drain and add the rice, three cups water and salt and cook till the rice is just done.

3. Heat the remaining ghee in another deep non stick pan. Add the cumin seeds, mustard seeds, chana dal, curry leaves and turmeric powder and sauté till the seeds splutter.

4. Add the rice and toss, taking care that the rice grains do not break.

5. Add lemon juice and toss again.

6. Serve hot garnished with a sprig of coriander leaves.

# Lasooni Naan

Garlic is a wonderful addition to any food, adding a spark of flavour and a whole new dimension to whatever food is being made. Lasooni Naan has plenty of golden fried garlic kneaded into the dough. And the end result is an extremely flavourful accompaniment that goes with practically every main dish on the menu. We have many orders for this as a starter too!

## Ingredients

3 cups refined flour (maida)

2 tablespoons fried garlic (see note below)

1½ teaspoons baking powder

1 teaspoon salt

2 teaspoons castor sugar

2 tablespoons butter

1 cup milk

¼ cup chopped fresh coriander leaves

Butter, as required

## Method

1. Set aside a little flour for dusting and sift the rest with baking powder and salt into a bowl. Add the castor sugar, butter and mix well. Add the milk and two tablespoons of water, fried garlic and coriander leaves and knead into a medium soft dough. Cover with a damp cloth and rest it for an hour.

2. Divide the dough into eight equal portions and roll into balls. Cover them with a damp cloth and rest for half an hour.

3. Preheat oven to 250ºC / 475ºF.

4. Roll out each ball, on a floured surface, into a five to six inch diameter disc. Pull it from one end to give it an oval shape. Place on a baking tray and bake in the preheated oven for seven to eight minutes.

5. Remove from the oven, apply butter and serve hot.

# Note

To make two tablespoons fried garlic, chop twenty five to thirty garlic cloves and fry them in two tablespoons of oil till brown.

# Dals & Accompaniments

# Dals & Accompaniments

# Dal Mizaaz

## Ingredients

¾ cup split skinless green gram (dhuli moong dal), soaked for ½ hour

¼ cup split pigeon peas (toor dal), soaked for ½ hour

½ teaspoon turmeric powder

**Salt to taste**

3 tablespoons butter

½ tablespoon cumin seeds

1 small onion, chopped

1 small tomato, chopped

15 garlic cloves, chopped

1 inch ginger piece, cut into thin strips

½ tablespoon coriander powder

½ tablespoon cumin powder

¼ tablespoon Khazana garam masala powder (see annexure)

½ tablespoon red chilli powder

¾ cup chopped fresh mint leaves

¼ cup chopped fresh coriander leaves

½ tablespoon lemon juice

**For garnish**

A sprig of fresh coriander leaves

A sprig of fresh mint leaves

Homely yellow dal redolent with the flavour of fresh mint - perfect with fluffy rice. It never fails to surprise a new guest and the regulars put it high on their 'must have' list! Besides toor dal is popular in India as a major source of protein and a staple food. The dried lentil is most often seen in home kitchens, but the fresh young pods are also used as a vegetable.

## Method

1. Drain and cook the two dals with two and a half cups water, turmeric powder and salt in a pressure cooker till pressure is released five to six times (five to six whistles).

2. Heat two tablespoons butter in a deep non stick pan. Add the cumin seeds and sauté till fragrant. Add onion and sauté till lightly browned.

3. Add the tomato and sauté until soft. Add the garlic and continue to sauté till browned.

4. Add the ginger strips and sauté for a minute. Add the coriander powder, cumin powder, garam masala powder, red chilli powder, quarter cup mint leaves and sauté for two minutes.

5. Add the dals, the remaining mint leaves and coriander leaves and mix well.

6. When the mixture comes to a boil, add salt, the remaining butter and quarter cup water. Mix and add the lemon juice and mix well.

7. Serve hot, garnished with fresh coriander and mint sprigs.

# Palak Chholay

## Ingredients

1 bunch (330 grams) spinach, blanched and chopped

1¼ cups (250 grams) chickpeas (kabuli chana), soaked overnight

2 teaspoons tea leaves

12 pieces dried Indian gooseberry (amla)

3 green cardamoms

1 black cardamom

2 bay leaves

1 inch cinnamon stick

2 tablespoon ghee

¼ cup oil

1 tablespoon cumin seeds

1 tablespoon dried fenugreek leaves (kasoori methi)

1½ inch ginger piece, chopped

15 garlic cloves, chopped

1 tablespoon green chilli paste

3 tablespoons chholay masala (see annexure)

1 tablespoon coriander powder

¾ cup fresh tomato puree

Salt to taste

2 teaspoons dried mango powder (amchur)

1 teaspoon Khazana garam masala powder (see annexure)

¼ teaspoon red chilli flakes

The ubiquitous chholay pumped up with iron - simmered in fresh spinach puree and spices. Have it piping hot with Lasooni Naan. As we do ask for feedback, patrons generally thank us for introducing them to a new combination! But did you know that chickpeas are not a modern-day food, but have been around for centuries?  Another interesting piece of news about it is that during World War I, ground-roasted chickpeas were used – and sometimes still are – as a substitute for coffee in Europe!

## Method

1.  Drain the chickpeas and put in a pressure cooker. Tie up tea leaves, amla, green cardamoms, black cardamom, bay leaves and cinnamon in a muslin cloth to make a potli and add to the cooker, along with five cups of water. Cook under pressure, on low heat, till pressure is released eight to ten times (eight to ten whistles).

2.  Open the lid when the pressure reduces completely, discard the spice potli, strain the chickpeas and reserve the cooking stock.

3.  Heat the ghee and oil in a deep non stick pan. Add the cumin seeds, dried fenugreek leaves, ginger and garlic and sauté for five minutes on medium heat.

4.  Add green chilli paste, chholay masala and coriander powder and sauté for five minutes.

5.  Add the spinach and tomato puree and cook, stirring, for seven to eight minutes or till dry and the oil separates.

6.  Add salt, dried mango powder, chickpeas and the reserved cooking stock and mix well.  Simmer for five minutes. Add garam masala powder and mix and cook for two minutes.

7.  Transfer into a serving bowl, garnish with red chilli flakes and serve hot.

131

# Lalla Mussa Dal

Kali dal in our signature style – it is our pride, but our neighbours' envy. How it got its name is another story altogether. One of the fastest moving items on our menu, on record days a couple of hundred litres dished out is normal! Ginger lends its special touch to this dish but do go easy with it... few people know that too much ginger can cause something called "ginger jitters", or ginger intoxication, when the nervous system is over-stimulated

## Ingredients

½ cup whole black gram (sabut urad)

⅛ cup whole green gram (sabut moong)

Salt to taste

2 green chillies, cut into thin strips

1 inch ginger piece, cut into thin strips

½ cup melted butter

¾ cup tomato puree

1 teaspoon Kashmiri red chilli powder

1 teaspoon coriander powder

¾ teaspoon roasted and crushed dried fenugreek leaves (kasoori methi)

½ cup fresh cream

1 tablespoon ghee

7-8 garlic cloves, finely chopped

For garnish

½ inch ginger piece, cut into thin strips

## Method

1. Mix together both grams and wash well at least four times in salted water. Drain, add one cup fresh water and soak for one hour.

2. Drain and boil in one cup of water till the scum surfaces. Collect the scum and discard. Strain the dals and put them into a pressure cooker. Add one cup fresh water, green chillies and ginger and cook under pressure on low heat till the pressure is released ten to twelve times (ten to twelve whistles).

3. Open the cooker when the pressure reduces, add quarter cup butter and simmer on low heat for forty-five minutes, stirring continuously and mashing with a wooden churner (mathni).

4. Heat the remaining butter in a deep non stick pan, add the tomato puree and sauté on low heat till fat rises to the surface.

5. Add the red chilli powder, coriander powder and kasoori methi and sauté for a couple of minutes.

6. Add the boiled dals and mix well. Add the cream and mix well.

7. Heat the ghee in a small non stick pan, add the garlic and sauté till brown. Add this to the dal mixture and mix well. Add one cup water and salt and let it come to a boil.

8. Serve hot, garnished with ginger strips.

# Punjabi Kadhi

## Ingredients

**For pakoras**

½ cup + 2 tablespoons gram flour (besan)

1 medium onion, finely chopped

⅓ cup chopped fenugreek leaves (methi)

1 inch ginger piece, grated

¾ teaspoon carom seeds (ajwain)

1 teaspoon red chilli powder

A pinch of baking soda

Salt to taste

Oil for deep frying

**For kadhi**

1 cup yogurt

¼ cup gram flour (besan)

1 teaspoon turmeric powder

Salt to taste

2½ teaspoons ginger-garlic paste

1 teaspoon green chilli paste

2 tablespoons oil

¾ teaspoon fenugreek seeds (methi dana)

½ teaspoon cumin seeds

4-5 black peppercorns

6 dried red chillies, halved

5-6 cloves

A pinch of asafoetida

1 medium onion, sliced (optional)

½ inch ginger piece, chopped

1 teaspoon red chilli powder

At home we cook this kadhi practically every week, but usually minus the deep fried pakode. But here we give you the traditional kadhi with pyaaz methi pakode. Yogurt is an all-purpose and totally healthy food, by itself or incorporated into dishes. It is a good low-fat substitute for cream, can be used to thicken curries, works as a gentle yet efficient meat tenderiser and has more health benefits than could be believed!

## Method

1. Heat sufficient oil in a kadai to fry the pakoras.

2. Mix the gram flour, onion, fenugreek leaves, ginger, carom seeds, red chilli powder, baking soda and salt. Add half cup of water and mix into a soft dough.

3. Drop small portions of the gram flour mixture into the hot oil and deep fry till golden. Drain on absorbent paper and set aside.

4. For the kadhi, whisk the yogurt and gram flour well together ensuring that there are no lumps. Add turmeric powder, salt, ginger-garlic paste, green chilli paste and three cups of water and whisk again.

5. Heat the oil in a deep non stick pan, add fenugreek seeds, cumin seeds, black peppercorns, red chillies, cloves and asafoetida and sauté for half a minute. Add the onion (if using) and ginger and sauté for a minute.

6. Add the yogurt mixture and mix well. When the mixture comes to a boil, simmer on low heat, stirring occasionally, for fifteen minutes.

7. Add red chilli powder and fried pakoras and continue to simmer for four to five minutes.

8. Serve hot with steamed rice.

# Aloo Pyaaz Ka Raita

It's simple, it's tasty and it compliments any main course.  It's important to choose the right type of potatoes, the best ones to use for boiling are the 'waxy' ones. They contain relatively high levels of moisture and sugar, but are fairly low in starch content and will hold their shape well when cooked.

## Ingredients

1 medium potato, boiled, peeled and cut into small cubes

1 medium onion, chopped

1¾ cups yogurt, whisked

½ teaspoon roasted cumin powder

Salt to taste

For garnish

A pinch of roasted cumin powder

A pinch of Kashmiri red chilli powder

## Method

1.  Keep aside a little onion and potato for garnish and mix the rest with yogurt, roasted cumin powder and salt in a bowl.

2.  Transfer into a serving bowl, garnish with the reserved onion and potato cubes.  Sprinkle a pinch of roasted cumin powder and Kashmiri red chilli powder on top and serve chilled.

# Mint Chutney

It is as tasty as it is nutritious and, what's more, it goes well with just about anything. Chutneys are a common accompaniment and come in a huge variety. They may be sweet or hot, or somewhere in between, but they always stimulate the appetite!

## Ingredients

1 cup fresh coriander leaves

1 cup fresh mint leaves

1 small onion, chopped

2 green chillies

½ teaspoon black salt

1 teaspoon crushed roasted cumin seeds

Salt to taste

¼ cup yogurt

2 tablespoons dried pomegranate seeds (anardana)

4 garlic cloves

## Method

1.  Grind the coriander leaves, mint leaves, onion, green chillies, black salt, cumin seeds, salt, yogurt, anardana and garlic with five teaspoons of water to a fine paste.

2.  Transfer into a small bowl and store in a refrigerator.

3.  Serve as an accompaniment.

# Bhindi Raita

The skill is in cutting the bhindi as thinly as possible and then the raita becomes a visual delight. Also known as lady's finger or okra, they originally came from West Africa and the fruit - which is what we are familiar with - is used in some form or the other almost all over the world.

## Ingredients

200 grams ladyfingers (bhindi), cut into thin diamond shaped slices

**Oil for deep frying**

1¾ cups yogurt, whisked

**Salt to taste**

½ teaspoon roasted cumin powder

¼ teaspoon black salt

Kashmiri red chilli powder to sprinkle

## Method

1. Heat sufficient oil in a kadai and deep fry the ladyfingers till crisp. Drain on absorbent paper and set aside to cool.

2. Whisk together yogurt, salt, cumin powder and black salt in a bowl.

3. Transfer into a serving bowl, add the fried ladyfingers, mix gently, sprinkle red chilli powder on top and serve chilled.

# Sweet Imli Chutney

A favourite of young and old - this sweet and sour chutney can be well described in one word - versatile. It goes with so many things and is a must for all types of chaats.

## Ingredients

1¼ cups grated jaggery
1 cup tamarind (imli)
2 tablespoons dried ginger powder (soonth)
¼ cup raisins
1 tablespoon red chilli powder
1 teaspoon turmeric powder
Salt to taste
1 tablespoon coriander powder

## Method

1. Heat two cups of water in a deep non stick pan. Add jaggery and cook till it melts.
2. Add tamarind, dried ginger powder, raisins, red chilli powder, turmeric powder, salt and coriander powder. Mix well.
3. Add eight cups of water and cook for forty to forty five minutes or till tamarind is soft.
4. Remove from heat when the mixture is thick. Strain the mixture and set aside to cool.
5. Serve with starters.

# Sweets

# Sweets

# Kesar Pista Kulfi

Kulfi was once the dessert of the rich, eaten during the summers, when the body and the soul needed cooling off. Today, it is a haute favourite the world over. A wonderful dessert, especially during the hot summer months! The origins of kulfi date back to the Mughal era, when the emperors were pampered with this cold delight. From being once reserved exclusively for royalty, kulfi is now a popular street food in India.

## Ingredients

A generous pinch of saffron
2 tablespoons crushed pistachios
1 litre (5 cups) full-fat buffalo milk
5 crushed green cardamoms
2 tablespoons crushed cashewnuts
2 tablespoons crushed almonds
½ cup condensed milk
1 tablespoon cashewnut paste

## Method

1. Bring the milk to a boil in a deep non stick pan. Add crushed green cardamoms and simmer on low heat, stirring, for twenty five to thirty minutes, or till it is reduced to half its original volume.

2. Add crushed cashewnuts, pistachios and almonds and mix well and continue to simmer.

3. Remove the cardamom skins and continue to simmer for twenty minutes or till it is reduced to one third its original volume.

4. Add condensed milk, saffron and cashewnut paste and mix well. Remove the pan from heat and set aside to cool.

5. Pour into kulfi moulds and keep in the freezer to set for six to eight hours.

6. Unmould and serve.

# Chocolate Mousse

Okay, so you thought chocolate made you fat, even as it made you happy, right? That may be true if you eat too much of it, but a little every day will not only make you feel good emotionally, but also physiologically. This perfectly sweet, perfectly creamy, perfectly chocolaty is indeed a perfect dessert for entertaining. Prepare it one day in advance and set as individual portions to avoid arguments.

## Ingredients

1 cup roughly chopped dark chocolate

3 egg yolks

2½ teaspoons castor sugar

⅛ cup milk

⅔ cup fresh cream

½ cup chocolate chips

## Method

1. Cook the egg yolks and castor sugar in a double boiler, stirring, till thick or till it coats the back of the ladle.

2. Heat the milk in a non stick pan and add the egg-sugar mixture and mix well.

3. Place the chocolate in a bowl and pour the milk-egg-sugar mixture over it and mix till the chocolate melts.

4. Whip the cream lightly and fold into the chocolate mixture.

5. Pour this mixture into a piping bag and half fill four shot glasses. Sprinkle some chocolate chips on top and pipe some more chocolate mixture over the chips.

6. Sprinkle more chocolate chips on top and keep the glasses in a refrigerator to set.

7. Serve chilled.

# Lychee Phirni

Lychees lend their own special flavour to this popular north Indian dessert. When the fruit is not in season, you can use the tinned variety.

## Ingredients

300 grams canned lychees, chopped

1 litre (5 cups) milk

2¾ tablespoons Basmati rice, soaked and coarsely ground

6 tablespoons grated mawa / khoya

⅛ cup sugar

½ teaspoon green cardamom powder

A few drops rose water

12 almonds, slivered

12 pistachios, slivered

## Method

1. Boil the milk in a deep non stick pan for ten minutes, stirring continuously so that no skin forms on the surface.

2. Add the coarsely ground rice and cook, stirring occasionally, till the rice is cooked.

3. Add the khoya, sugar and lychees and stir. Cook for two minutes.

4. Add the green cardamom powder and rose water. Mix and take the pan off the heat.

5. Cool the phirni and pour into individual serving bowls, preferably kasoras (earthenware bowls). Sprinkle almond and pistachio slivers, chill and serve.

# Gulab-e-gulkand

The goodness of gulkand ensconced in traditional gulab jamuns – a sweet surprise. We are not always taken aback when someone reports that the idea has been copied by the neighbourhood halwai!

## Ingredients

125 grams hariyali khoya / mawa

60 grams cottage cheese (malai paneer)

3½ tablespoons refined flour (maida)

3½ tablespoons cornflour

6¼ teaspoons candied rose petals (gulkand)

¼ teaspoon green cardamom powder

1½ cups sugar

1 teaspoon milk

Ghee for deep frying

1 tablespoon rose water

## Method

1. Grate the khoya and paneer separately and mix.

2. Keep aside two tablespoons of the mixture and add the refined flour and cornflour to the rest and knead well till smooth. Divide into twenty five equal portions.

3. Add the gulkand and green cardamom powder to the reserved khoya-paneer mixture and mix well. Divide into twenty five equal portions and roll into balls.

4. Take a portion of the khoya-paneer mixture in your palm, make a dent in the centre and place the khoya-gulkand filling inside. Bring in the edges to cover the filling, press and roll into a smooth ball. Ensure there are no cracks on the surface.

5. Boil together the sugar and one and a half cups water, stirring till the sugar dissolves. Add the milk, and when the scum rises to the top, skim it off. Simmer till the syrup turns a light golden. Add rose water and mix. Keep the syrup warm.

6. Heat sufficient ghee in a kadai on medium heat. Gently slide in half the khoya balls. Lift the kadai off the heat and rotate it gently till the balls start to float to the top.

7. Place the kadai back on the heat and continue to fry on a medium heat, stirring gently, till the balls turn golden brown in colour.

8. Drain and dip the balls in the syrup. Let them soak for at least fifteen minutes before serving.

9. Serve warm or cold.

# Kesari Indrayani

Rasmalai goes regal: small chenna balls plumped up in saffron milk. What I love about this dessert is that it looks and tastes superb and belies the simple method of preparation. It is also great to make when you have many people to entertain.

## Ingredients

A few saffron strands mixed with 1 tablespoon of warm milk

1 medium watermelon

1 medium musk melon

1 large papaya

1 large apple

9 red grapes

500 grams angoori rasmalai

½ cup milk

20 green grapes

## Method

1. Using a parisienne scoop, make thirty five round balls from the watermelon, twenty five from the musk melon, thirty five from the papaya and thirteen from the apple. The remaining portions of each fruit can be used to make some other dish.

2. Keeping four red grapes for garnish, cut the remaining into round slices.

3. Place the angoori rasmalai in a large bowl. Add milk and mix gently. Add all the fruits, including green grapes, and mix gently again.

4. Transfer this into four martini glasses and drizzle the saffron milk on top. Decorate the rim of each glass with a red grape and chill before serving.

# Gil-e-firdaus

A gift from the nizami kitchens of Hyderabad - kheer in contemporary style: rice, doodhi and rose, our in-house specialty. Rose petals not only impart a pleasant aroma, but are also extremely therapeutic and have been used in traditional medicine for many centuries.

A healthier option for this dessert is to use brown rice in place of white. We do recommend it highly to whoever asks for suggestions.

## Ingredients

½ cup grated bottle gourd (lauki/doodhi)

1 tablespoon ghee

¼ cup rice, soaked, drained and crushed1

litre (5 cups) milk

5 green cardamoms

6 crushed almonds

6 crushed cashewnuts

2 tablespoons dried rose petals

¼ cup grated mawa/khoya

½ cup sugar

1 tablespoon rose water

## Method

1. Heat the ghee in a non stick pan, add the bottle gourd and sauté till all the moisture dries up. Add the rice and sauté for five minutes.

2. Add the milk and cook, stirring continuously for ten minutes.

3. Peel the cardamoms and crush the seeds and add to the pan and continue to cook, stirring, for ten to fifteen minutes.

4. Add the almonds, cashewnuts and dried rose petals and mix well.

5. Add the khoya and stir to mix well. Add the sugar and cook, stirring, for ten minutes or till all the sugar dissolves.

6. Add the rose water and mix well.

7. Pour into kasoras (earthenware bowls) and cool. Serve chilled.

# Measurements

| Ingredient | Quantity/No | Weight | Ingredient | Quantity/No | Weight |
|---|---|---|---|---|---|
| Almonds | 10 | 15 gms | Cottage cheese (paneer), grated | 1/2 cup | 70 grams |
| Almonds | 1 cup | 140 grams | Crisp puri (papdi) | 24 | 72 grams |
| Apple1 medium | 120 grams | | Cumin powder | 1 teaspoon | 3 gms |
| Asafoetida (hing) | 1 teaspoon | 4 gms | Cumin seeds | 1 teaspoon | 3 gms |
| Asafoetida (hing) | 1 pinch | 0.25 gram | Cumin seeds | 1 tablespoon | 9 grams |
| Baby corn | 10 | 125 grams | Curry leaves | 10 | 1 gram |
| Baby potatoes | 10 | 200 grams | Dried fenugreek leaves (kasuri methi) | 1 tablespoon | 1 gm |
| Baking powder | 1 teaspoon | 3 gms | Dried mango powder (amchur) | 1 teaspoon | 1 gm |
| Baking soda (soda bicarbonate) | 1 teaspoon | 4 grams | Dried red chillies | 10 | 20 grams |
| Basmati rice | 1 cup | 200 grams | Fennel seeds (saunf) | 1 tablespoon | 9 grams |
| Bay leaf | 1 | 0.4 gram | Fennel seeds (saunf) | 1 teaspoon | 3 gms |
| Bay leaves | 10 | 4 grams | Fennel seeds (saunf) powder | 1 teaspoon | 3 gms |
| Beetroot, medium | 1 | 145 grams | Fenugreek seeds (methi dana) | 1 teaspoon | 5 gms |
| Black cardamoms | 11 | 10 grams | Fenugreek seeds (methi dana) | 1 tablespoon | 12 grams |
| Black pepper powder | 1 teaspoon | 3 gms | French beans | 10 | 75 grams |
| Black peppercorns | 1 cup | 100 grams | Fresh coriander leaves | 1 cup | 25 grams |
| Black salt | 1 teaspoon | 5 grams | Fresh coriander leaves | 1 tablespoon (chopped) | 5 gms |
| Boneless skinless chicken breast | 1 | 65 grams | Fresh cream | 1 cup | 200 mls |
| Bottle gourd (lauki/doodhi) | 1 medium | 500 grams | Fresh cream | 4 tablespoons | 60 ml |
| Bottle gourd (lauki/doodhi) | 1 small | 250 grams | Fresh fenugreek leaves | 1 small bunch | 175 grams |
| Breadcrumbs | 1 cup | 110 grams | Fresh fenugreek leaves | 1 medium bunch | 250 grams |
| Breadcrumbs | 2 tablespoons | 12 grams | Fresh fenugreek leaves | 1 large bunch | 580 grams |
| Brinjal (bharta), large | 1 | 630 grams | Fresh green peas (shelled) | 1 cup | 150 gms |
| Brinjal (bharta), medium | 1 | 460 grams | Fresh mint leaves | 1 tablespoon chopped | 4 grams |
| Brinjal (bharta), small | 1 | 275 grams | Fresh mint leaves | 1 cup | 30 grams |
| Brinjal, medium | 1 | 30 gms | Fresh scraped coconut | 1 cup | 120 gms |
| Broccoli, small florets | 5 | 15 grams | Fresh scraped coconut | 1 tablespoon | 5 grams |
| Butter | 1 tablespoon | 15 gms | Fresh spinach leaves | 1 small bunch | 150 grams |
| Butter, melted | 1 cup | 200 grams | Fresh spinach leaves | 1 medium bunch | 250 grams |
| Button mushrooms | 10 medium | 125 grams | Fresh spinach leaves | 1 large bunch | 450 grams |
| Caraway seeds (shahi jeera) | 1 teaspoon | 3 gms | Fresh tomato puree | 1 cup | 235 grams |
| Carom seeds (ajwain) | 1 teaspoon | 2 gms | Fresh yeast | 1 tablespoon | 10 grams |
| Carrot, medium | 1 | 90 gms | Frozen green peas | 1/2 cup | 80 grams |
| Carrot, small | 1 | 50 grams | Garam masala powder | 1 teaspoon | 2 gms |
| Cashewnut paste | 1 cup | 225 gms | Garlic | 10 cloves | 15 gms |
| Cashewnut paste | 1 tablespoon | 15 grams | Garlic paste | 1 tablespoon | 15 gms |
| Cashewnuts | 10 | 20 gms | Ghee | 1 tablespoon | 15 grams |
| Castor sugar | 1 cup | 125 grams | Ghee | 1 cup | 210 grams |
| Cauliflower, medium | 1 | 500 grams | Ginger | 1 inch piece | 10 grams |
| Chaat Masala | 1 teaspoon | 1 gm | Ginger paste | 1 tablespoon | 15 grams |
| Chickpeas | 1/2 cup | 100 grams | Gram flour (besan) | 1 tablespoon | 5 gms |
| Cinnamon | 1 inch stick | 0.5 gram | Gram flour (besan) | 1 cup | 100 gms |
| Cloves | 10 | 1 gm | Green capsicum, medium | 1 | 125 grams |
| Coconut milk | 1 cup | 200 mls | Green capsicum, small | 1 | 98 grams |
| Coriander powder | 1 teaspoon | 2 gms | Green cardamom powder | 1 teaspoon | 2 gms |
| Coriander powder | 1 tablespoon | 6 gms | Green cardamoms | 10 | 3 grams |
| Coriander seeds | 1 teaspoon | 2 grams | Green chilli | 1 | 2 grams |
| Coriander seeds | 1 tablespoon | 6 gms | Green chilli paste | 1 teaspoon | 5 grams |
| Corn kernels | 1 cup | 150 grams | Green grapes | 10 | 30 gm |
| Cornflour | 1 tablespoon | 5 gms | Honey | 1 tablespoon | 15 mls |

# Measurements

| Ingredient | Quantity/No | Weight |
| --- | --- | --- |
| Hung yogurt | 1 cup | 275 grams |
| Indian gooseberry (amla) | 1 | 35 grams |
| Jaggery, grated | 1 cup | 200 grams |
| Jaggery, grated | 1 teaspoon | 10 gms |
| Jaggery, grated | 1 tablespoon | 30 gms |
| Ladyfingers | 40 medium sized | 300 grams |
| Lemon juice | 1 teaspoon | 5 ml |
| Lemon juice | 1 tablespoon | 15 mls |
| Mace (javitri) | 2 | 3 grms |
| Mace (javitri) powder | a pinch | 0.08 gram |
| Mawa/khoya | 1 cup | 180 gms |
| Mawa/khoya, grated | 1 tablespoon | 20 gms |
| Melon seeds (magaz) | 3 tablespoons | 30 grams |
| Milk  1 cup | 200 mls | |
| Minced mutton (keema) | 1 cup | 250 grams |
| Mustard seeds | 1 teaspoon | 4 gms |
| Mustard seeds | 1 tablespoon | 10 grams |
| Onion seeds (kalonji) | 1 teaspoon | 3 grams |
| Onion, large | 1 | 110 gms |
| Onion, medium | 1 | 90 gms |
| Onion, small | 1 | 60 gms |
| Pistachios | 20 | 10 gms |
| Pistachios | 1/4 cup | 30 grams |
| Pomegranate pearls (taza anar) | 1 cup | 180 grams |
| Pomegranate pearls (taza anar) | 1 tablespoon | 10 grams |
| Pomegranate seeds (anardana) | 1 teaspoon | 3 grams |
| Pomegranate seeds (anardana) | 1 tablespoon | 10 grams |
| Pomfret, medium | 1 | 220 grams |
| Poppy seeds (khus khus) | 1 teaspoon | 4 gms |
| Poppy seeds (khus khus) | 1 tablespoon | 12 grams |
| Potato, large | 1 | 150 grams |
| Potato, medium | 1 | 100 grams |
| Powdered sugar | 1 cup | 125 gms |
| Prawns,  medium | 24 | 250 grams |
| Prawns, large | 24 | 360 grams |
| Prawns, small | 30 | 250 grams |
| Raisins (white, black) | 10 | 5 grams |
| Raisins (white, black) | 1/2 cup | 90 grams |
| Raisins (white, black) | 1 teaspoon | 5 grams |
| Raisins (white, black) | 1 tablespoon | 10 grams |
| Red capsicum, medium | 1 | 125 grams |
| Red chilli flakes | 1 teaspoon | 1 gm |
| Red chilli paste | 1 teaspoon | 7 grams |
| Red chilli powder | 1 teaspoon | 3 gms |
| Red chilli powder | 1 tablespoon | 10 grams |
| Red chilli powder | 1 cup | 100 grams |
| Red grapes | 25-30 | 290 grams |
| Red kidney beans (rajma) | 1 cup | 185 grams |
| Refined flour (maida) | 1 cup | 120 grams |
| Refined flour (maida) | 2 tablespoons | 15 grams |

| Ingredient | Quantity/No | Weight |
| --- | --- | --- |
| Rice | 1 cup | 200 gms |
| Roasted chana dal (daalia) | 1 cup | 130 grams |
| Roasted cumin powder | 1 teaspoon | 3 grams |
| Roasted peanuts | 2 tablespoons | 18 grams |
| Roasted peanuts | 1/4 cup | 30 grams |
| Rose syrup | 1 tablespoon | 15 mls |
| Salt | 1 teaspoon | 5 grams |
| Sambhar onions | 10 | 80 grams |
| Semolina | 1 cup | 200 gms |
| Sesame seeds (til) | 1 tablespoon | 15 grams |
| Sesame seeds (til) | 1 teaspoon | 5 gms |
| Split Bengal gram (chana dal) | 1 teaspoon | 5 grams |
| Split Bengal gram (chana dal) | 1 cup | 200 grams |
| Split black gram with skin (chilkewali urad dal) | 1/2 cup | 100 grams |
| Split lentils (masoor dal) | 1 tablespoons | 15 grams |
| Split pigeon pea (toor dal/arhar dal) | 1 cup | 200 grams |
| Split skinless black gram (dhuli urad dal) | 1 teaspoon | 5 grams |
| Split skinless black gram (dhuli urad dal) | 1 tablespoon | 15 grams |
| Split skinless black gram (dhuli urad dal) | 1 cup | 200 grams |
| Split skinless green gram (dhuli moong dal) | 1 cup | 200 grams |
| Spring onions bulbs | 2 | 20 grams |
| Spring onions with greens | 2 | 100 grams |
| Star anise (badiyan/phoolchakri) | 2 | 4 grams |
| Sugar | 1 tablespoon | 15 grams |
| Sugar | 1 cup | 250 grams |
| Sugar | 1 teaspoon | 5 gms |
| Tamarind pulp | 1 teaspoon | 5 gms |
| Tamarind pulp | 1 tablespoon | 20 grams |
| Tomato, large | 1 | 110 grams |
| Tomato, medium | 1 | 95 grams |
| Tomato, small | 1 | 60 grams |
| Turmeric powder (haldi) | 1 tablespoon | 9 gm |
| Turmeric powder (haldi) | 1 teaspoon | 3 gms |
| Vinegar | 1 tablespoon | 15 mls |
| Walnuts | 1 cup | 120 grams |
| White pepper powder | 1 teaspoon | 3 gms |
| White sesame seeds | 1 cup | 160 grams |
| White sesame seeds | 1/4 cup | 35 grams |
| Whole black gram (sabut urad) | 1 cup | 250 grams |
| Whole dried red chillies | 8 | 10 grams |
| Whole green gram (sabut moong) | 1 cup | 240 grams |
| Whole wheat flour (atta) | 1 cup | 150 gms |
| Yellow capsicum,  medium | 1 | 125 grams |
| Yellow capsicum,  small | 1/4th | 60 grams |
| Yogurt | 1 cup | 250 gm |

# Tips

- A few pieces of tender raw papaya added to meat while cooking helps to soften it.
- A good and instant substitute for khoya can be prepared by mixing two tablespoons gram flour, half a cup milk and one tablespoon fresh cream.
- A little lemon juice added to beetroot will deepen the red color.
- A little oatmeal added to soup will not only thicken it but also add flavour and richness.
- A pinch of turmeric powder and a teaspoon full of ghee added to half a cup of dal before pressure-cooking it will give it a better flavour.
- Add a cupful of soaked poha to five cupfuls of rice while soaking for idlis and grind. You will get softer and lighter idlis.
- Add a few drops of lemon juice while preparing sugar syrup. The impurities will collect on the surface of the syrup, which you can then remove.
- Add a few pieces of raw mango while cooking bitter gourd. It will not only remove the bitterness but also add to the flavour of the curry.
- Add a little sugar to the dosa mixture to make them brown and crisp.
- Add a pinch of asafoetida to a teaspoonful of ginger juice. Add this mixture to a curry, to obtain the flavour of onion, without putting onions in the curry.
- Add a pinch of turmeric powder to the oil before adding green vegetables. The vegetables will retain their green color better even after cooking.
- Add a small piece of beetroot while making tomato puree; it will give it a bright red color.
- Add a walnut while grinding mint chutney. The chutney will taste better and will not become watery.
- Add half a cup of yogurt to the onions being fried for making curries. Yogurt gives a good texture and taste to the curry. It is also a good substitute for tomatoes.
- Adding a little cornstarch to gram flour while mixing the batter gives crisper pakodas.
- Adding acidic ingredients like lemon juice, vinegar, tomatoes, ketchup or wine to beans at the end of the cooking time will make them firm.
- Adding carom seeds to any fish preparation is beneficial since its strong flavour reduces the fishy smell of the dish. It is especially helpful in fish that are deep-fried dipped in batter.
- After frying paneer, put the hot pieces in salted cold water. These pieces should be added only at the final stages of the dish. This will keep them soft and prevent them from getting rubbery.
- After shelling peas, wash the pea pods thoroughly. Add salt and pepper and pressure-cook. Cool, mash and sieve, to make a delightful cream of pea soup. You can also make soup of carrot and beetroot skins.
- After stuffing capsicums and tomatoes, arrange in a muffin tin before placing them in the oven. They will stay upright and keep their shape perfectly. You could also do this with baked apples or other round or stuffed items.
- Always warm dry spices like cumin seeds, cardamom, cloves, etc. on a griddle before powdering. They will grind faster and the powder will be finer.

# Tips

- Any wada mixture should be beaten well with hand prior to frying. This incorporates air in the batter and makes it light.

- Avoid reheating green vegetable dishes to retain their color.
  Before using mustard oil for preparing vegetables etc., heat it to a point till light smoke emerges from it. This would remove the pungency from the oil.

- While buying brinjals ensure they are smooth to the touch and light in weight. Heaviness indicates that they are over mature with plenty of seeds inside.

- Buy mushrooms from a reputed store. They should be white, firm and odourless. Use mushrooms as soon as you buy them. They do not refrigerate well.

- Chapattis would come out very soft if a little rice flour is used while rolling out the dough.

- Chop green chillies, etc. either with a steel knife or steel scissors. Do not use iron knives since the paste will tend to turn blackish later on.

- Crush vermicelli or sago and roll patties or croquettes in this powder before frying, to get a crisp crunchy cover.

- Curry leaves used in any dish are usually discarded. So in about one-two spoons of oil, fry washed curry leaves till crisp. Crush with hands. Store this curry powder in an air-tight bottle and use it to flavour gravies, chutneys, idli batter, etc.

- Cut tomatoes vertically instead of horizontally, to keep the slices firm and retain much of their juice.

- Do not add saffron directly to a dish. Infuse threads in a little hot water or milk for at least five minutes before adding it to a dish. This will bring out its flavour and ensure even coloring.

- Do not panic if you have added too much turmeric in the vegetable. Cover the vessel with a white muslin cloth. It will absorb the excess turmeric.

- Do not use fresh pineapple in gelatin-based desserts. Fresh pineapple contains an enzyme that prevents gelatin from setting. Use canned pineapple instead or boil the fresh fruit with sugar for ten minutes before adding to dessert.

- Excess tomato puree may be frozen in an ice cube tray. Remove frozen cubes and store in a sealable freezer bag, using as and when required.

- Foods that have to be deep-fried should not be too cold and must be added in small batches so that they do not lower the temperature of the hot oil.

- For flaky paranthas add ghee instead of oil to the flour while kneading the dough.

- Grind dry pomegranate seeds coarsely before adding in any food preparation.

- Having ready dry mint powder is handy for pulaos, kababs, parantha stuffings and raitas. Place two cups of mint leaves on a baking tray and roast in an oven at 100°C for 45-50 minutes. Cool and crush into a powder. Can be stored for a long time in an airtight bottle.

- If dosa sticks to the tawa, rub an onion cut into half dipped in oil on the hot tawa and sprinkle some water over it. Now try making the next dosa.

- If onions are not cooked well in any preparation, not only does it give a smell of raw onions but the dish also spoils faster.

# Annexure

### Garam Masala Powder

Dry roast one after the other10-12 blades of mace, 8-10 one-inch cinnamon sticks, 25 cloves, 25 green cardamoms, 10-12 black cardamoms, 2 nutmegs, 8-10 bay leaves, 8 teaspoons cumin seeds and 4 teaspoons black peppercorns till fragrant and transfer into a bowl. Set aside to cool. Grind the roasted spices to a fine powder. Transfer into a bowl and when cooled store in an air tight container.

Makes 1 cup

### Chaat Masala

Dry roast one after the other 4 tablespoons coriander seeds, 2 teaspoons cumin seeds and 1 teaspoon carom seeds (ajwain) on a non stick pan till lightly browned and fragrant. Transfer into a bowl, mix and set aside to cool. Grind them with 2-3 dried red chillies, 3 tablespoons black salt, ½ teaspoon citric acid, 1 teaspoon dried mango powder, 1 tablespoon salt and 1 teaspoon black pepper powder to a fine powder. Transfer the powder into a bowl and set aside to cool.

Store in an air-tight container.

Makes ½ cup

### Pav Bhaji Masala

Dry roast ½ teaspoon black peppercorns, 12 Kashmiri dried red chillies, 2 tablespoons cumin seeds, 2½ tablespoons coriander seeds, 6 one-inch cinnamon sticks , 1 teaspoon salt, ¼ teaspoon black salt, 25 cloves, 1 black cardamom, 6-8 curry leaves, 2 bay leaves and 1 tablespoon fennel seeds on low heat for five minutes. Add 1½ tablespoons dried mango powder (amchur), mix well and set aside to cool completely. Grind to a smooth powder. Store in an airtight container when completely cooled.

Makes 60 grams

### Chholay Masala

Dry roast 2 tablespoons cumin seeds, 3 tablespoons coriander seeds, 2 one-inch cinnamon sticks, 8-10 cloves, 1 black cardamom, ½ teaspoon carom seeds (ajwain), 2½ teaspoons black peppercorns, 1 teaspoon dry fenugreek leaves (kasoorimethi), 3-5 tirfals, 2 tablespoons dried pomegranate seeds (anardana), 8-10 bay leaves and 8-10 dried red chilliesin a non stick pan till fragrant.Transfer the mixture onto a plate and set aside to cool. Grind with 1 teaspoon dried mango powder (amchur), ½ teaspoon dried ginger powder (soonth), 1 teaspoon salt and 2 teaspoons black salt to a fine powder.Cool and store in an airtight container.

Makes ¾ cup

### Kadai Masala

Coarsely grind together 4 tablespoons coriander seeds, 20-25 black peppercorns, 7 green cardamoms, 2 dried red chillies, 1 black cardamom and 1 tablespoon cumin seeds.

Makes 7 tablespoons

### Achari Masala

Coarsely grind together 1 tablespoon mustard seeds, 1 tablespoon onion seeds (kalonji), 1½ tablespoons fennel seeds (saunf), ½ teaspoon fenugreek seeds (methidana), 2 tablespoons coriander seeds and 1 tablespoon cumin seeds.

Makes 10 tablespoons

# Annexure

### Kaju Magaz Paste
Boil ½ cup cashewnuts (kaju) and ½ cup melon seeds (magaz) in 1½ cups water for five minutes. Drain, cool and grind with ½ cup water to a fine paste.

Makes 1 cup

### Biryani Masala (Hyderabadi Dum Gosht Biryani)
Grind together 3 one-inch cinnamon sticks, 15 cloves, 25-30 black peppercorns, 30 green cardamoms, 3 black cardamoms, 4 star anise (badiyan), 2 tablespoons caraway seeds (shahijeera), 8 bay leaves, 2 tablespoons coriander seeds, 3 dried red chillies, 2 blades of mace (javitri) and ¼ teaspoon nutmeg (jaiphal) powder.

Makes 13 tablespoons

### Biryani Masala (Murgh Noormahal Biryani)
Grind together ⅛ cup green cardamoms, 3 blades of mace (javitri), 10 cloves and 2 one-inch cinnamon sticks to a powder.

Makes 5 ½ tablespoons

### Fried Garlic
Chop 25-30 garlic cloves and fry them in 2 tablespoons of oil till brown.

Makes 2 tablespoons

### Mussallam Masala
Grind together 10 green cardamoms, 2 black cardamoms, 2 one-inch cinnamon sticks, 1 tablespoon black peppercorns, 1 tablespoon coriander seeds, 4 cloves, 1 tablespoon caraway seeds (shahi jeera), 1 tablespoon fennel seeds (saunf), 1 mace blade and 2 tablespoons dried rose petals.

Makes 30 grams

# Glossary

| English | Hindi | English | Hindi |
|---------|-------|---------|-------|
| Almonds | Badam | Green gram | Sabut moong |
| Apple | Saeb | Green grapes | Hare angoor |
| Apricots | Aloo Bukhara | Green peas | Hara matar |
| Asafoetida | Hing | Honey | Shahad |
| Barley | Jau | Hung yogurt | Chakka |
| Bay leaves | Tejpatta | Indian salmon | Rawas |
| Beetroot | Chukandar | Ladyfingers | Bhindi |
| Bengal gram | Chana | Lemon | Nimboo |
| Black cardamom | Badi elaichi | Melon seeds | Magaz |
| Black gram | Saboot urad | Minced mutton | Keema |
| Black pepper powder | Kali mirch powder | Musk melon | Kharbooj |
| Black peppercorn | Kali mirch | Mustard oil | Rai ka tel |
| Black salt | Kala namak | Mustard seeds | Rai |
| Bottle gourd | Doodhi/lauki | Nutmeg | Jaiphal |
| Brinjal | Baingan | Onion | Pyaaz |
| Button chillies | Boria mirch | Onion seeds | Kalonji |
| Candied rose petals | Gulkand | Pistachios | Pista |
| Caraway seeds | Shahi jeera | Prawn | Jheenga |
| Carom seeds | Ajwain | Raisin | Kishmish |
| Cashewnut | Kaju | Raw papaya | Kachcha papita |
| Castor sugar | Pisi chini | Red capsicum | Lal Shimla mirch |
| Cauliflower | Phoolgobhi | Red chilli flakes | Kuti hui lal mirch |
| Chickpeas | Kabuli chana | Red grapes | Lal angoor |
| Cinnamon | Dalchini | Refined flour | Maida |
| Cloves | Laung/lavang | Roasted chana | Daalia |
| Coconut | Nariyal | Saffron | Kesar |
| Colocassia roots | Arbi | Scraped coconut | Kasa hua nariyal |
| Coriander seeds | Sabut dhania | Screw pine water | Kewda jal |
| Corn | Makai | Silver foil | Chaandi ka warq |
| Cottage cheese | Paneer | Split Bengal gram | Chane ki dal |
| Cumin seeds | Jeera | Split black gram with skin | Chilkewali urad dal |
| Curry leaves | Kadhi patta | Split green gram with skin | Chilkewali moong dal |
| Dried fenugreek leaves | Kasoori methi | Split pigeon peas | Arhar dal/Tuvar dal |
| Dried green gram dumplings | Mangodi | Split skinless black gram | Dhuli urad dal |
| Dried Indian gooseberry | Sookha amla | Split skinless green gram | Dhuli moong dal |
| Dried mango powder | Amchur | Spring onion bulb | Hara pyaaz |
| Dried pomegranate seeds | Anardana | Star anise | Badiyan/phool chakri |
| Fennel seeds | Saunf | Stone flower | Dagad phool |
| Fenugreek seeds | Methi dana | Tamarind | Imli |
| French beans | Farsi | Turmeric powder | Haldi powder |
| Fresh coriander leaves | Hara dhania | Vinegar | Sirka |
| Fresh fenugreek leaves | Methi | Watermelon | Tarbooj |
| Fresh mint leaves | Pudina | White sesame seeds | Safed til |
| Fresh spinach leaves | Palak | Whole wheat flour | Atta |
| Gram flour | Besan | Yam | Suran |
| Green capsicum | Hari shimla mirch | Yeast | Khamir |
| Green cardamom | Chhoti elaichi | Yellow capsicum | Pili shimla mirch |
| Green chilli | Hari mirch | Yogurt | Dahi |